Be Better Broken:
In Service to Liberation

By Yaffa

ISBN (paperback): 979-8-9925727-9-7

ISBN (ebook): 979-8-9949096-0-7

First paperback edition February 2026

Book cover and design by Sheyam Ghieth

Line Edited by Mays Salamah

Foreword by Ijeoma Oluo

merajpublishing.com

To the Broken, may our sharp edges tear apart what should never have been—may they move us to a liberated world.

<u>Other titles by Yaffa:</u>

Blood Orange

Desecrated Poppies

Inara: Light of Utopia

Sage

Whispers Beneath the Orange Grove

Living to 99

Letters From a Living Utopia

Thistle

5

THE HOPE OF ACHIEVING JUSTICE TOMORROW ALLOWS US TO SURVIVE TODAY

Foreword by Ijeoma Oluo

As I write this foreword, another person has been murdered by ICE agents for trying to save a woman from their brutality. I write this foreword as genocide rages on in Palestine, in Sudan, in Congo—with no outrage on our part to match its murderous fury.

It is hard to write, hard to teach, hard to organize in these times. It can seem futile. It can seem like we are not only repeating ourselves, but repeating generation after generation of people trying to find a way to say simply that we deserve to live free.

And so I'm sitting down today to write this foreword because I must, because it is hard. And when it is hard that is when it is needed more than ever. But because it is hard and because it is so necessary, I am picking each word with even greater care.

I want to throw care out the window. I want to divorce my rage from the love that bore it and unleash it on those who are hurting us. I want to unwind my years of somatic therapy work that gave context and meaning to my pain and become a tornado that takes down all around me.

But I am respectfully listening to my rage and listening to where it tells me it must go instead of where I want it to go. I am reciting to myself the promises I have made to this work and the people who do it with me. And I will also cry. I will yell. I will do what I must as a human being with a human response to such cruelty and violent oppression in the world. But I will always get back to the work, because the work is nonnegotiable.

I am honoring my commitment to liberation and to the work and words that can help shine a light on our path to it.

We are traumatized people working with traumatized people, doing work that further traumatizes us, in a world that refuses to recognize that trauma. And because of this, true care is often cast aside. I'm not talking about capitalist ideas of care that have us taking spa days. I'm not talking about colonialist ideas of care that have us isolating from our people and cutting ourselves off from the suffering of our neighbors.

I'm talking about how we care for each other, how we care for ourselves, and most importantly: how we care for the work.

When I met Yaffa in person for the first time, after being connected online for a while, I was struck first by their care. Care in the small gift of healing tonics they gave to me as we met at a small coffee shop. Care in how they listened to my and my partner's stories, and care in what they shared with us. And as we later sat onstage together and talked liberation, I was once again struck by Yaffa's care.

Care is not always soft. Care can be a fierce, firm thing. Often care must be. And as Yaffa spoke of what the fight for liberation looks like to them, I was able to see Yaffa's care in their anger and heartbreak, in the way they intently listened to every audience question, in every word chosen, and every action and idea discussed on how we can be more free.

Care can feel slow, it can feel like a hindrance at a time like this. But when our oppressors care so little in their violence, we must care even more.

Yaffa talks of writing this book at a time of great hurt, hurt that came from community that was supposed to care. That lack of care did not just harm individuals, it harmed the work. Even though Yaffa and I do our work in different places and with different methodologies, their description of this harm resonated deeply with me. I have experienced similar harm, and I don't know any liberation workers who haven't. The harm done by those who do this work without care is devastating. This is harm that can destroy movements with precision our oppressors could only dream of. We deserve so much more than what even we are willing to give ourselves.

Care is hard when we are broken. Care is hard when we aren't given a quiet place to heal. Care is hard in a world that says that because we are broken, we shouldn't have to care. That it is too much to ask.

And it is a lot to ask: to be broken and to keep being broken and to still care about how that brokenness shows up in our fight for survival. It is a lot to ask to be accountable for the harm we cause when our own harm still feels so fresh. But we must, because we are all broken. And when we are broken we cannot become unbroken, we can only become something new. We must take great care in what we decide to become.

START WITH 'I AM THE PROBLEM'

Introduction

I struggle to begin writing this book. Many of my books are born from rage and frustration—rage at systemic oppression, frustration with those who uphold it—including my own people.

This book is no different. But the weight feels heavier because the starting point is my people, not the systems.

It feels as though 2025 is the year I am meant to process my frustration and resentment toward my people—something I do not do lightly, because it feels like attacking an inherent part of myself.

I ask myself, again and again, who am I to speak about this? And yet the universe keeps pushing me toward writing and speaking, reminding me that this is the work I have dedicated my entire life to.

I do not work to fix privileged individuals rooted in systems of oppression. My work has always been for my people. And without having these conversations, we risk repeating the same harmful patterns that pull us deeper into systems of oppression.

I have spent decades practicing conflict transformation and transformative justice, long before I had the language for either. I have supported hundreds of communities in building values-aligned practices, and I have watched them fracture again and again. But this book is not about conflict alone—I have written extensively about conflict in previous works.

I was initially trained in conflict resolution and taught others through peer support frameworks. But as I went deeper into the work, I realized conflict resolution did not reflect the practices I grew up with in my Palestinian and Muslim communities, nor among other marginalized communities surviving the united states.

Even as a child, I knew we did not resolve conflict—we transformed it. Conflict resolution, as I was trained, often felt like a strategy to avoid disposability. But in my community, there was no disposability. We were families torn apart by war, genocide, and fascism. We were all broken—and we cared for one another.

Care failed when conflict resolution was applied without transformation.

Years later, I gained language for what I had always known: liberatory relationships require accountability. Accountability requires addressing root causes of harm. Conflict resolution is not accountability—it is, at best, an entry point. A step before accountability, if I am being generous.

Accountability leads to growth. Growth is the priority. Without it, we cannot continue caring for one another in liberatory ways.

Later still, I learned about conflict transformation—a practice that centers root causes. And then transformative justice, something I had witnessed as a child and mistakenly believed was universal.

In my community, adults gathered to address harm. Involving the state was never an option—the harm would always outweigh any benefit. Responsibility belonged to the community.

That remains my favorite part of transformative justice: responsibility is collective, not individual. No one in a community bears zero responsibility for what occurs within it. When we accept that, we can transform everything—not just pass the spotlight of blame from one person to another.

This book is about responsibility. About healing. About hearts. About being generative. About being irrelevant. We have much work to do before we can truly embody liberatory practice. Without shared responsibility for our healing and growth, we will never move toward a liberated world.

This book was sparked by community violence—three incidents across three countries, on a single day in August 2024. There has been community violence before and since, but August 9th, 2024 holds a permanent place in my memory.

I am in Falasteen, driving from Haifa to Bethlehem. We are preparing to meet with political prisoners and to launch a campaign to rebuild homes demolished near Bethlehem. The day begins early. News arrives of conflict in Cairo—the kind that behaves like a forest fire, indiscriminate and consuming everything in its path.

The second incident unfolds in Europe during the two-hour drive. This one is quieter, more contained, but deeply sinister. There is no explosion, no dramatic collapse—just a swift, lethal blow to years of work. The kind of harm that corrodes relationships for years.

The two comrades I am traveling with go into a meeting while I work from a café, trying to support from a distance. Then the third incident arrives, in the form of a text: *"Hey, can we talk when you have time?"* I know immediately that everything is about to change. And it does.

By the time I fully understand what has happened, we are having dinner with political prisoners, strategizing next steps. I step away to address the situation, but the damage has already been done. A best friend is on suicide watch. The infrastructure I built so that the work could continue beyond me is fractured.

The funds to begin rebuilding the first house are now delayed. The money for fire extinguishers to stop settlers' arson attacks in Al-Khalil (Hebron) is delayed. Funding for gender-affirming surgery for a trans comrade is delayed. All because one person was unwell.

Almost everyone who knew responded the same way: *"Well, they're not okay."* As if being unwell absolved harm. Only after that did people ask about those impacted—as though they were an afterthought, the person who caused harm always centered first. As if individual actions do not have long-term consequences in other people's lives.

I write this by the Mediterranean, on the one-year anniversary. The work has not recovered. The people impacted have not recovered. All because a single person was "not okay," because a single person was not better broken.

Being broken is political when it is synonymous with marginalization, while being whole is synonymous with privilege. When we view trauma as the tool that breaks and violence the poison that escapes we reinforce white supremacist narratives. Violence is always political: who enacts violence and who receives the violence are political. How we reach the state of violence is political and instrumental to oppression. How we respond to violence is worldbuilding, either moving us towards fascism or towards liberation.

How we interact with violence is political, because how we react to violence is defined by likability politics which are defined by systems of oppression. If we like you we can overlook almost anything. If we've never liked you we will not overlook any violence, even the absence of violence is not enough to protect you.

Meeting violence with violence is political under the guise of community safety — I am not saying there is no role for violence in liberation work, I am saying community violence towards one another in response to state violence we do not know how to process is political. Resistance violence is also very obviously political.

Likeability is political. We like those that systems of oppression have told us to like: folks with charisma, power, and those we have deemed as our community — all defined by systems of oppression, even when that likability is transferred through a shared identity of marginalization.

There are so many facets of violence that demand entire books written about them and there are some brilliant books out there that discuss them such as any book by Mariam Kaba; I also recommend *Beyond Survival,* co-edited by Ejeris Dixon and Leah Lakshmi Piepzna-Samarasinha as a great entry into concepts like Transformative Justice.

This book is in response to one response to community violence in particular. A response that infuriates me to no end. When someone within community causes harm there are too many who will say

"Well, they're broken. They're not okay."

What a disgustingly degenerative response to harm. How dare you.

Of course, this is not the response to when the most marginalized of the most marginalized cause harm. This is when the more privileged of the marginalized cause harm, when they are liked due to charisma, power, or whatever else that made them popular.

It infuriates me — all things that are not generative infuriate me. This in particular infuriates me enough to launch a podcast, write a book, and make shirts with these words.

I acknowledge that none of us are okay, that we are all broken. How dare you use that as an excuse for violence—whether as the person committing the violence or the bystanders?

This statement is told to people who have experienced violence.

I experience far too much community and state violence to capture in a single book or to even publicly share and acknowledge or even process in my own mind. When the violence is relevant enough and I tell others, it is rare to receive a response different than the one above. At times it is the response above until the individuals themselves experience similar violence, and then they recognize that uttering these words out loud in response to someone informing you about harm is moving us towards fascism. You can reflect on your intention for these words in hell or as you read this book, whichever comes first.

This response and this justification need to go.

Your being broken is irrelevant in a world where we are all broken. Enacting violence is a choice that we control as individuals, pretending otherwise is from the deepest parts of fascist systems.

To use being broken as an excuse for your violence is the same as anglo-europeans using harm against them as justification for slavery and colonization or zionists using the holocaust as justification for genociding Palestinians, or cis people claiming fear is their reason for transphobia and wanting to genocide transness.

It is ludicrous, ridiculous, and nonsensical. So stop it.

Be better broken.

No more excuses. Be better broken. We cannot afford anything less.

I ask you to open yourself to this work—to read with the assumption that every word in this collection is about you. It is not. But without that openness, it becomes nearly impossible to discern which parts are, and which are not about you as an individual embedded in community.

But being better broken is not enough. What matters is what we do once we are better broken.

Some would say—and I am one of them—that being better broken means standing for and actively building toward a collectively liberated world. Not everyone agrees, so let me be clear: your brokenness is irrelevant to me if it does not serve collective liberation.

For too long, whiteness has framed healing as an individual pursuit rather than a communal responsibility. In the global north, healing often means responding to community harm by pushing people further into individualism. Community *can* be harmful—especially in societies built on stolen land and sustained through colonization and abuse. But individualism does not heal that harm.

Many healing practices over the last twenty years have treated individualism as the solution, failing to recognize that it is precisely this individualism—produced by oppressive systems—that leads to harm in the first place.

Being better broken without contributing to a collectivist vision of liberation is not liberation at all. It is merely fragmentation—shattered pieces held together by the very systems that broke us.

To be better broken is to claim responsibility for liberation and to move toward it through service. Being in service is what matters to me. I want people to experience joy, peace, love—but if it all ends with you, you are not my priority. My priority is service to collective liberation.

Be better broken so you can be in better service.

My methodology for being better broken stems from my no waste philosophy. I witnessed my grandfather reuse everything for his garden, composting without ever calling it compost. During my engineering program they wanted to frame it as sustainability, without ever acknowledging that our indigenous communities have never wasted. Freshman year we learned about the concept of cradle to grave, and in my resistance against the elitist education I was receiving that believed that whiteness would save the planet, I finally found language for the practices I grew up with and have always known. As I moved into mental health, death and birthing work, and social and environmental justice organizing I learned to utilize the same practices; no waste could be applied to every aspect of life. No waste has been a necessary philosophy in my practice for healing, self-actualization, and liberation.

This book was originally two books—one about being better broken, and one about being in service. I merged them because the moment demands both, and because I believe there are people ready for both. I also do not have the capacity to tour two books in 2026. Merging them was an act of accessibility—for myself and for others.

My work across organizing, training, incubation, mobilizing, and publishing is about preparing for the next crisis. I hope you read this book with that in mind. The next crisis is always closer than we think.

Let's build infrastructure where we are prepared for the next crisis.

Let's build a world where the next crisis never happens.

Be better broken.
Be in service to collective liberation—and everything it requires.

WE ARE ALL BROKEN

BE BETTER BROKEN

Be Responsible Broken

I was four when Mama gave my older sister, who was five at the time, a time out. In my mind E was locked away forever and needed rescuing. I went outside, through the garden and found the window to the room she was being held in. I tell E I will rescue her. I try to find a way into the window; albeit on the ground floor, it is still a challenge.

I did it anyway. I climbed the tree despite my fear of heights. I held onto the bars of the window that would have actually made it impossible to enter the room from the outside without cutting the metal anti-theft bars. I held on and when I looked inside she was gone.

I thought she had been killed. *Mama had killed her* and I was already mourning her in the garden when what felt like hours later (probably minutes) I found E playing with the neighbor's kid. Mama had let her out but E did not think I should be told while on my rescue mission. E also refused to let me play with them after.

I learned certain things really early in my life.

> I learned that violence and death impacted my family.

> I learned that I am able to play a role in helping others.

> I learned that responsibility is not always shared.

I learned that being responsible can not be in exchange for gratitude or personal benefit after, for we can't guarantee those things.

I learned that supporting others would not make them like me.

I learned that I would do it anyway.

I learned that responsibility meant being a part of the story, a commitment to truth, care, and love.

I am grateful that I learned these things early on. I am grateful that I inherited Mama's anxiety. I am grateful that I was not celebrated for being responsible and I still continued to be responsible.

The memory above will be seen as traumatizing to most people and elicit a sympathetic reaction towards me. I am grateful for that and will not deny that this memory for years was a source of pain. Now though, in a *no waste* practice, where I claim and learn from every experience, I see it for what it is. I take from the memory the lessons for the future and leave behind the rest. I take lessons of responsibility, gratitude, and understanding who I have always been.

This experience was a moment where I was broken in a multitude of ways, and yet instead of turning my back on responsibility I chose to continue being responsible, even before I knew what that word meant.

Part of my journey is also witnessing others with similar breakage not be responsible. Growing up my sisters were not always the most responsible. They would often disappear and it would be my responsibility to figure out where they disappeared to as Mama freaked out. Even as we grew older, they did not always claim responsibility in their relationships and paths in life, sometimes going as far as blaming me for their actions — often blaming me.

In many ways, they needed to be better broken. In many ways, some of them still do.

But they taught me a valuable lesson. Being broken has little relevance when it comes to responsibility and those who say otherwise to avoid responsibility and accountability are doing just that, avoiding responsibility and accountability. Everything impacts us, our trauma and things that have broken us surely play a role in every part of our lives, but they do not define who we are, they do not define whether or not we will be responsible.

The same experience above could have been my justification for never being responsible for my sisters or anyone else. But that's not what happened. This experience also did not do the opposite. As traumatic as it was, it didn't impact whether or not I was responsible.

It did impact how I communicated, how anxious I was, how I internalized that I am not worthy; but it didn't make me turn my back on responsibility. Perhaps it was the fact that I was told as soon as I was born that I had responsibilities, that I needed to be a main character who took care of those around me. Perhaps it was my cancer moon. Perhaps it's my Leo Sun, rising, Mercury, and Venus that made me a nurturer. It could have been anything, there are a thousand pathways and the important part is that I understood the assignment. Not everyone who is told to be responsible becomes responsible. Not every Cancer Moon or Leo Sun knows to be responsible.

In many of the spaces I am in (more in spaces I am not in) people will use the violence they have experienced as justification for ways that they might be showing up. In the end of the day I do not care that because of your childhood trauma you ended up getting someone deported. You got someone deported — that is all. You should not have done that. You need to be accountable for your actions.

Part of your accountability could be to acknowledge that your pain influences how you respond to situations and find ways to move past it so it never happens again. We're all broken here. Be better broken.

In my years as an organizer, particularly in what's known as the united states, I have seen people's actions leading to our community members getting killed, incarcerated, deported, hospitalized, unhoused, and displaced from community (and all the things that happen in between this list). I myself have experienced the last three things from that list while being put at risk of incarceration and deportation by community members.

Like I mentioned in the introduction, it is rarely the most marginalized of the most marginalized who are using being broken as an excuse for these actions and are not the ones causing these forms of harm. It's usually the people with enough access to assimilation, marginalized or not, that are the most violent and the ones who justify their violence. They are also the ones with enough likability politics for others to justify their actions on their behalf by saying "but they're broken" as if being broken forces people to get others deported and/or killed.

We have all messed up and caused harm, it is a part of being alive and in relationship with others, land, spirit, and everything else in existence. There is a spectrum though, and the larger the harm the greater the accountability. Our actions are ours. Our pain is ours too. We are responsible for how we move in this world. We are responsible for the world we are trying to build.

Responsibility does not end with ourselves.

If, as I was trying to rescue my sister I end up accidentally killing the tree I climbed or fell and broke a bone, then I am responsible for killing the tree or harming my body. If that had happened my mom would have also been responsible, especially considering she was the only adult in the situation. If this was a situation of domestic violence and other adults left us to endure it then they are also responsible. The responsibility ecosystem is endless and so is the accountability.

We are constantly growing, and moving towards becoming all that we are meant to be. Even the most harmful things can offer great lessons. It was the harm that I endured from those who called themselves community members that moved me towards accountability practices through conflict transformation and transformative justice.

Without responsibility we can not uncover all the areas that need to be dismantled around us and all the growth that's possible. We limit ourselves when we're not responsible.

Many are taught to avoid responsibility. If we avoid responsibility then we do not have to carry the weight of accountability and ultimately growth.

Recently, at a workshop about community care, this came up. We were talking about how many communities will put a single or a few community leaders on a pedestal and want to follow them entirely. I am a Leo, so I love pedestals but that's not the problem. The problem is placing only a few individuals on pedestals instead of everyone claiming a pedestal to do better. Elevating a person is a way to avoid responsibility. When they mess up they are exclusively to blame. When growth is needed they have to grow. Often, the individuals do not even feel responsible for placing this individual in this position in the first place.

This is different from saying that at different times we will have different leaders and we are responsible for them and ourselves. It is our responsibility to ensure we have the best leadership for the moment. It is also our responsibility to step up or down depending on the moment, changing our roles often *in service* to liberation.

I learned this my freshman year of university, during my very first group project. I did not want to lead, even though I was the right fit. Instead, I elevated the student that had the most knowledge about the project but didn't have experience leading. It was a disaster and I learned that sometimes you have to step up even when you don't want to for a greater purpose.

Everything is a responsibility.

Our wellbeing, how we treat others, our roles in life, the world we're attempting to build, everything is a responsibility.

I recently received a message from someone who came after me last year, leading to a friend ending up in suicide watch and in a mental health program for a month; loss of another friend; four key individuals fully leaving the pro-Palestine movement (which nearly destroyed the infrastructure that enables me to get resources to queer and trans folks impacted by genocide); delayed rebuilding a house for a Palestinian family; and delayed and jeopardized someone's gender affirming surgery—and none of that includes the harm to me.

'I'm sorry if I harmed you.'

No mention of the friend they harmed, no mention of the work they harmed, no mention of any accountability or reflection on how they showed up at all.

But they're not the only one who needs to claim responsibility. The vast majority of people's reactions to the situation was to say "well they're broken/not okay". They are a large part of the inspiration for this book.

Then, there is my own accountability.

I put people in harm's way by centering and befriending this person.

I must be responsible for the infrastructure I could have fortified further.

Responsibility shows up in my mindfulness for the future, it shows up in my work that gets fortified, it shows up in how I invite folks into spaces.

Being responsible and accountable is not a way to say I am a bad person. They are ways to grow and do better, because we deserve better. My brokenness taught me this, it didn't move me away from responsibility and accountability.

Following someone taking accountability, we are responsible for being open to accepting that accountability. This person is not disposable, no one is disposable. I may be hurt but it is my responsibility to nurture a liberatory space where we can all return after we have messed up and are accountable.

There is another layer that surrounds this situation and that's the responsibility for the world we're building. In my case it's responsibility for collective liberation. This incident hurt in ways I have yet to process, but it did not stop my work because I am not doing this for this individual or any other community member. I am doing it because I am responsible for my role in building a collectively liberated world. Most people do not move past interpersonal responsibility, refusing to do the uncomfortable labor that responsibility demands.

We will not build a liberated world without shared responsibility for it. Do you claim responsibility for building a liberated world? What I mean by that is not "are you *okay* with a liberated world or do you stand against fascism?" I'm not referring to being here for liberation on the weekend or you organize with your friends occasionally. I mean have you claimed responsibility for a collectively liberated world with every inhale and exhale?

Without responsibility we limit ourselves.

We are beautifully expansive beings, our motivations and purposes are not the same — pretending otherwise can be deadly.

Being broken does not, or at the very least should not, make us irresponsible.

At worst, make brokenness irrelevant, at best, use the brokenness to connect with responsibility within and beyond yourself.

Why waste brokenness? When everything can be used to propel us towards liberatory practice, why waste anything?

Being responsible for our collective liberation means that we're responsible for our actions, for understanding and claiming our power, and for our healing and knowing how our brokenness is impacting how we're showing up.

We must claim responsibility; we must be responsible broken.

I EXIST
IN THIS MOMENT
IN THIS BODY
FOR A
PURPOSE

Be Heart Broken

Are we born with hardened hearts?

Most people will say no immediately. My autism would ask when is born? Which heart? What is hardened?

I ask the first of the four questions because I am thinking of the concept of breaking.

I visualize a vase in the solid material sense shattering.

From an emotional and spiritual lens I visualize a heart breaking, shattering and scattering.

In the way my mind's eye makes sense of this my autism wonders where the shattered glass goes, what was in the vase? What was in the heart?

In the physical realm the glass is spread within a specific distance dictated by physics. Whatever the vase is filled with prior to shattering is spread, guided by the same principles of physics. But the heart is not guided by the concepts of physics, shattering and spreading into an unknown distance. I'm curious about this distance in a way that might validate why I became an engineer. More importantly, I'm curious about what's inside.

Did you know the heart — the organ — is surrounded by a membrane called the pericardium? Did you know that in Chinese medicine the pericardium is an organ? I've been sitting with this awareness for years, wondering if maybe when we say a heart breaks or opens we are talking about the pericardium and not the organ itself. I wonder if maybe there's an emotional/spiritual equivalent. I also wonder if there is a difference between opening and breaking, for is the result not the same? What was once inside is allowed to move freely now?

But what is inside?

I've been thinking about this concept since I was a child. Most of my life I have been afraid of what is inside. Growing up and into adulthood I related most to The Dark Phoenix from X-Men. I related to the idea that within me there is an uncontrollable limitless power that destroys everything. I was fourteen when I watched *X-Men: The Last Stand* when The Dark Phoenix is the central character.

Since then, I have explored the comics as well, which presents a more nuanced vision of The Dark Phoenix.

In the movie, The Dark Phoenix is a source of uncontrollable destruction. In the comics, it is unlimited power, it is neither good nor bad. But I didn't have that to relate to, I related to the destruction.

I believed that if I let you in, what's inside me will destroy you. If I let it out, it will destroy everything. This was reinforced daily with my family and in a society that did not know how to hold someone like me. I was wrong—not when I did anything wrong, I was just wrong. So I hid what's inside, allowed it to fester and grow, and then I became terrified of what it would come out as. The Dark Phoenix also needed to be contained, keeping what's inside locked away—otherwise the consequences were immense. Too many children are taught that we are wrong for any reason—in my case it was too neurodivergent, too disabled, too brown, too loud and too quiet, too trans, too Muslim, too Palestinian and not Palestinian enough.

Over the years I have learned that just because we fear something does not mean it's true, and just because we destroy does not mean we are unjust. A lot in our society must be torn down, burned away to make way for what is to come.

But I didn't know that as a child or early into my adulthood. Over time, I learned it is not just the fear of what is inside, it is specifically the fear of loss of control.

What is inside our hearts feels controlled within a hardened exterior, held behind the pericardium, released little by little. If there is no vessel there is no control, and without physics who am I to know how many timelines and realms I could tear apart?

The endlessness of spirit is terrifying in a world where we are taught we must control.

But we know control isn't real. The idea that we control whether or not a heart breaks is ludicrous. The idea that we control what's in a heart to begin with is ridiculous. The idea that we control what happens in a closed or shattered heart is nonsensical.

I am a living being, a part of all spirit that flows in this and every realm, in every timeline. I am a part of an ecosystem that I can not comprehend until I return to source. I exist in this moment within this body for a purpose, always moving towards source. I control my actions, but everything beyond that is not mine. Even my actions are debatable when I can not control anything around me.

It fascinates me that we view hearts breaking or anything breaking as an end. Sure someone took time to create a glass vase, fill it with water or whatever else, and now it shatters and someone needs to clean it up (all within the constraints of physics). But the vase is now endless, losing its constraints that were placed upon it. Sure, it is no longer a vase, but who said sand wanted to be confined in the first place?

If our hearts are filled with the parts of us that are closest to source then is breaking a release of the magic that we are, allowing us to move closer to oneness? Am I closer to myself and community when I am no longer confined?

What's confining me? What's telling me that I must stay confined? Am I actually confined?

I ask again, are we born with hardened hearts? What was that process like? Here's where we move away from the metaphor of a vase, for a vase is made by design, it is not a natural hardening process.

When something hardens in nature it is not smooth and perfectly rounded necessarily. When something hardens in nature it can have sharp edges, the outsides resembling thistle, thorny and sharp, beautiful and untouchable. Other times it's like a cactus plant, fruit ripe with nutrients but painful to reach.

There are some of us who have a shield around us, there are others who have thorns to keep others away. We are all on a spectrum somewhere, until we are one again with source.

If we do not control breaking and unbreaking then have we made them more relevant than they are? Do we know when they are beyond a hypothetical occurrence that we give power to?

I think a lot about hearts breaking because of how prevalent we use the concept. Many individuals will say their hearts are breaking witnessing genocide. Many will say their hearts are breaking when community or state violence occurs. Often, the concept is passive, like it's something that's happening to us and is an end. As if because our hearts have broken we can never be whole.

In the ways I think of hearts opening I actually don't think we can be whole when we are not broken. Our hardening due to systemic oppression is not natural, through breaking we return to ourselves and each other in a way that's difficult with hardened shells that pierce one another.

The truth is we're all broken — constantly in a state of breaking, but some breaks are complete and others are partial. Our edges might cause friction with one another as we're building relationships and community, leading to immense community harm and fracturing our movements.

Claiming our hearts breaking allows us to access space to learn to be with one another, offering grace, and possibilities for what's possible.

I only write these words because of the weaponization of the concept of breaking. I would love to live in a world where my writing is exclusively to satisfy my brain's curiosity around language and physical/metaphysical/spiritual concepts. Instead, I write and speak about this because there are consequences to how we claim our breaking.

Until we learn to claim being broken and move beyond the imperialist narratives of what it means to be broken we won't know how to build liberatory relationships to move towards a collectively liberated world.

May our hearts break, and may we have all that we need to claim the universe within us.

TO BE HUMAN IS NOT COMPATIBLE WITH WHITE SUPREMACIST CAPITALISM

Be Powerful Broken

Hurt People Hurt People.

What a horrific saying. In its simplicity it creates guardrails for possibility and a non-generative way to claim that being broken results in violence always.

It's true though, hurt people hurt people but that's only because every human in existence is hurt and they have hurt people. The truth is still weaponized.

This statement is often used as a weapon against those who have been hurt the most, as if hurt is not universal.

As a victim of childhood sexual assault one of my biggest fears was that I would somehow become a rapist myself. Everything in society told me I would, that I had no control over it. As if by having an experience it sits dormant in our bodyminds, taking over our subconscious and then just like that, one day it would take over our lives and we're helpless to it. What a disgusting way to view those at the margins and who have experienced such horrific pain throughout our lives.

Abuse does not beget abuse, even when the root causes of the violence have never been addressed.

Abuse does not define how we live our lives. We are not helpless to our brokenness and our experiences. These narratives are harmful and are often repeated in hundreds of different ways even by those who stand against them. It was in social justice movement spaces that this was weaponized around me most. We must do better, we must be better broken.

When we are taught that our legacy is a legacy of violence then when it happens we accept it as a natural part of being.

I was talking to a comrade earlier and mentioned a conflict that had come up several months ago that was resolved with relative ease. They laughed, saying that when another person had told them about the same conflict it was used as an example to uphold the "reality" that even people trained in conflict resolution and transformation will not be able to effectively move through conflict. We will all find our way to conflict. We actually very much should claim conflict, as conflict is what allows us to grow. The comrade was never told that the conflict was resolved; in fact, it was weaponized to uphold a narrative that conflict is violent and we are all going to be violent. This messaging is harmful and ultimately only upholds systemic oppression.

Conflict is natural, moving through conflict is natural. Violence is not natural. Just because violence can occur during conflict does not change the natural elements of conflict.

Violence is about power. Abuse is about control.

Hurt people hurt people.

But what happens if hurt people do not have power?

Hurt people hurt people.

If hurt people hurt people, and violence comes from power, then if an individual is powerless they can not be violent.

What we're actually saying here is the experience of violence makes us violent, but if we do not have power then we can not enact this prophecy, and can not in fact be abusive.

Thus, if we move away from power then we will not be violent, we will not abuse others.

Power is the problem.

All of the above is false.

Power is not the problem. Powerlessness does not make us safe.

As a culture worker, when I think of a phrase like *hurt people hurt people* I think about the cultural impact this has on liberation work. If we believe that our legacy is to harm the community because we have been harmed then the most marginalized (the most harmed) are seen as a liability and/or will avoid community as a form of harm reduction. But we yearn for community, and one of the pathways when we believe the above is to move towards powerlessness to be safe for our community.

I am in a lot of places with a lot of people who would like to pretend as if they do not have power, as if we **all** do not have power.

When we claim we do not have power then we claim that we can not be harmful; but to claim that we do not have power is like claiming we do not have oxygen as we continue to breathe. It is a blatant lie and in my opinion a violent one. A person who claims to have no power is a person that is violent in my opinion, because they will exert power over others unknowingly. Because power is constant. To be human is to be powerful.

When I train individuals on navigating and claiming power, I simplify power into two structures: power due to systemic oppression and inherent power. Many have studied the first part, recognizing privilege and marginalization within systems of oppression. Power analysis usually stops here.

I will often ask, were we powerful before systemic oppression? Will we be powerful in a liberated world? The answer is always yes. So, what is that power?

There is a wealth of power that exists outside of systemic oppression, far greater than anything systems of oppression can grant. The narrative that only systems of oppression can grant and take away power is a form of abuse to maintain dominance—and it is not true.

When some people want to pretend they have no power what they are saying is that they are embarrassed of the power they have from systems of oppression and/or want to avoid responsibility for their role in liberation work. Here's the reality: power due to systemic oppression is undeniable and denial is a way of trying to find a way out of doing the work to dismantle these systems. Denying power is violent. Every single human, regardless of levels of marginalization, carries power from systemic oppression—every single one. Power due to systemic oppression is fleeting, based on a reward system, and is capped depending on the identities we carry and the time and place we exist in during any moment of our lives. Power due to systemic oppression is not sustainable, nor is it reliable, shifting from moment to moment.

Inherent power on the other hand is human. It is human to love, to connect, to wonder, to dream, to build, to inspire. Inherent power does not fluctuate, even though it might feel like it fluctuates drastically. What actually fluctuates is how we claim inherent power. Every human is meant to be a connected and loving being; the building blocks are all within us. Systemic oppression creates barriers between us and the well of our being. The well does not change, and we all have access to it by virtue of being human. At the same time, I do not deny the long-term consequences of being barred from accessing our humanity. I wonder what this does to our DNA over generations? Will there come a day when all of us forget what it means to be human?

To me, to be human is the most powerful thing, but often to be human is seen as weak. Within capitalism and other systems of oppression we are tasked with moving away from our humanity to assimilate into the systems. Starting at home, even before school, we are taught that we must be strong to survive in this world. To be kind is to be called naive.

Even legacies of imperialism are blamed on us: to be generous is to be victim-blamed for settler colonialism.

To be loving is to be a fool. We are taught as children to cut off the parts of us that are human, because to be human is not compatible with white supremacist capitalism.

So many messages: to be human is to be weak, to be hurt is to hurt others, to be powerful is always violent.

At the same time we often see violent individuals as individuals who feel weak. We say cis-men are violent to partners because the rest of the world has taken their power away. Even with children, we say a boy has a crush on you when he threatens your safety, that he's too weak for his emotions.

If to be human is to be weak and if violence also comes from weakness then to be human is to be violent.

The contradictions within these statements is where humanity begins. Because what is weak? We are taught weakness is bad, making us both violent and vulnerable to violence. We are taught that we need to have hard exteriors to survive—and there is some truth there because white supremacist imperialism is cruel. To be strong is to have barriers even from ourselves.

The etymology of weak is rooted in being malleable, open to growth and transformation. To be weak is to be human, but to be violent comes from white supremacist definitions of strength.

All these narratives built so deeply into our culture mean we are taught to use systemic power to cut off our inherent power to protect ourselves and ultimately have power over others.

There is some truth to violence stemming from power, but the type and source of power matter. To be violent is to have access to power that is not inherent, which is to say it is power that is not ours. Violence is from power taken from someone or something else, it is stolen.

Hurt People, hurt people.

Is to say that to be human is to steal power and then exert that power over another, as if we didn't spend millennia in tune with nature and one another as we built communities everywhere, balancing land, body, and spirit.

We are powerful. Where the power comes from matters, and it is undeniable that we all have stolen power—that is what makes a systemically oppressive society. Moving past the embarrassment of carrying power (and away from systemically oppressive messaging that tells us that to be powerful is to be a 'bad' person) we are then able to use power that is not ours to dismantle the systems that are robbing so many of it. And then we can utilize our inherent power to build a better world.

So many of us are taught that to be marginalized is to be powerless; to be broken is to be powerless. As if in our breaking we released our power to the ethers and are left hollow, a void. To me, to be better broken is to no longer be constrained by the barriers to our power.

Shatter me, allow me to access the entirety of the universe, something I can't do behind barriers constructed by systemic oppression deeming me only powerful when I assimilate through them.

But even when we do not assimilate into systems of oppression the power bleeds from those systems into our everyday lives; even if we would rather they did not. Everything within systemic oppression is a power transaction, everything a commodity, even marginalization.

So much of my power due to systemically oppressive systems comes due to my multi-marginalized identities. I am able to redistribute resources in the millions of dollars because of my marginalization, not in spite of it. This doesn't remove the brutal nature of marginalization, it just means that I know how to effectively utilize my power. This skill set is what makes me an effective organizer, mobilizer, culture worker, and artist. There is power in everything.

To be powerful broken is to be able to understand the infinite amount of power that exists within each of us, predominantly inherent power, topped with power from systemic oppression. Every part of systemically oppressive society will want us to buy into a vision of humanity that is powerless. This messaging is beaten in us through schooling, parenting, and then work. Left alone, we would claim our power. I am grateful that I was always a disliked child, by family and teachers, rarely having friends. I am grateful because I learned to see through these bars of being liked and disliked and that power runs far deeper than anything society can grant.

At 13 I planned to run away and needed to find a way to make money to be able to sustainably depart. That same week, the transphobe who wrote about a basic magical child hit a billion dollar net worth. If she could do it, why couldn't I? I love the thirteen-year-old who believed that at 13 they could write novels that will change the world and allow them to be free. I wrote my first novel in the two months that followed—in math class.

I did not make a billion dollars, but so what? These days I write more books a year than the transphobe has published in her entire life.

It's not a competition, I will never compete with transphobes who are so deeply in denial of their inherent power that they are nothing more than caricatures in service to fascism. I don't want a billion dollars gifted in exchange for my inherent power. Keep your money, keep your influence, you are momentarily relevant and then gone, back to the powerlessness you've created for yourself.

May we all be always powerfully broken.

EVERYTHING GETS HARDER THE LONGER WE WAIT

Be Resistance Broken

I wish that it was just me who is irritated by how individuals show up within organizing and community spaces. I only separate those two for your benefit, for I believe every community space is one of organizing if it is done properly. This is not saying that inherently people coming together is organizing. Organizing is organizing. Organizing is having the knowledge to move through chaos and come out with something that makes sense. I just can not comprehend people coming together and not walking away a little closer to a liberated world. Blame my autism but it does not make sense. Make it make sense, why else would we have a community space if we're not worldbuilding together? You're ridiculous!

A lot of people think that people coming together is resistance.

A lot of people think their existence is resistance.

Technically, they're not wrong — you are not wrong. Technically. But it's a technicality.

Anything can be and is resistance.

Fascism is resistance to something, it doesn't make it a good thing.

The reality is that everything in existence is resistance.

White supremacy resists a liberated world by creating the circumstances for oppression and fascism. Transphobia is resisting a world where we have autonomy. Genocide is resisting a world where we live in peace.

The questions are what and how are we resisting, not if you are resisting—or if your existence is resistance.

Some will argue that by being a marginalized person alive you are resisting. I hate to break it to you (I really do), capitalism needs us, your breathing alone is not anti-capitalist. For indigenous folks, yes, our existence is resistance against settler colonialism but that only goes so far when we become settlers ourselves. Yes, fascism wants to destroy everything human and magical about us but passive resistance is not the same as building a liberated world.

The point is yes, you are resistance, but the following questions still apply.

What are you resisting? How are you resisting?

An understanding of resisting systems of oppression requires a deep historical analysis of marginalization beyond single identities, beyond victimhood, and even beyond intersectionality as we currently frame it. Without this analysis we assume that all of us who are marginalized are resisting equally.

Being gay on Castro St. in San Francisco is not resistance. Going to a gay party and assimilating within capitalist ideals of joy is not resistance.

Girl, just say you want to go to a party, go to a party, your storytelling is not that creative. Tell me one more time how the party is your rest so you can continue your "work". Girl, showing up to a single protest is not work, go back to your tech job and pretend you're a good person. Party it up, do what you want, but let's not pretend you're liberating the world with that $17 cocktail.

I know resistance parties. I even know resistance orgies. Yes, people are creative when it comes to liberation, why aren't you?

Everything can be about liberation. My autism can not comprehend any part of life being not about liberation, but that's not usually the case. Usually liberation is a small subset of our lives that we maybe do when crisis occurs and/or on the weekends. When liberation is separated from the rest of our lives then our existence is predominantly about assimilating.

There are countless reasons why marginalized people choose to assimilate every single day — I get it, survival is hard and some days the little reward dangled in front of us is hard to say no to. I get it. But let's not lie to one another. Claiming your existence is the resistance we need is a way to avoid accountability for assimilating and gaslighting others and yourself into believing that you don't have to actively resist, that all forms of resistance are equal and valid. They are not.

Even when marginalized people find one another and build community we can either be moving towards liberation or assimilating into the systemic oppressive culture all around us. There is no guarantee that we are always moving towards liberation with our resistance.

Which is why what we are resisting and how are critical questions to ask in every space.

None of us are inherently "good" because we are marginalized. No single identity moves us closer to liberation. However, there are certain identities that are farther from assimilation. There is power in the space between assimilation and liberation. When we are farther from systems of oppression, and in particular when there are no pathways to assimilate, then many of us are forced to learn to navigate the world beyond these systems. I discuss this more in *in service to the most marginalized of the most marginalized* essay later in this book.

For the sake of an understanding of resistance and brokenness we must understand that brokenness does not inherently mean that we know how to liberate ourselves and each other.

But some of y'all want to pretend as if that is the case, like because we're traumatized we must know how to be liberated. As if just because you're shattered you must be the second coming of Christ or something.

Girl, the majority of people in the world are broken, that's what happens when like 100 billionaires colonize all land and resources.

If being broken made us better people we wouldn't be here and I definitely would not be writing this essay in Ciudad de Mexico watching a live concert (see, everything can be about liberation — it's at a restaurant and I also had food).

As I re-read and edit this essay I recognize that I am blending two different concepts in relation to resistance and brokenness. There is the individual culture we carry within each of us that is taught to us by systems of oppression and there is the culture of movement spaces that is meant to be liberatory but is often not.

I witness this everyday. Many assume that others yearning for liberation have done the reconditioning work to show up in liberatory ways. Many assume that a space where individuals who yearn for liberation coming together must be liberatory. Instead, we find the same culture of systems of oppression within our spaces and ourselves: one of disposability, self-hatred, inhumanity, victimhood, bad communication, distrust, systemically oppressive hierarchy (sometimes in the form of consensus decision making), and so many other things that we find in capitalist white supremacist patriarchal spaces.

I am not the only one irritated, though most people will not tell you of their irritation, instead they leave. So many feel disempowered and a sense of despair, thinking that a better world can't be possible if the spaces where we are supposedly building collective liberation are the way they are.

There is a reason that state agencies infiltrate our spaces and destroy the culture.

We are the practice of utopia, and when our practice of utopia becomes white supremacy, people fall away, moving to hopelessness and disempowerment.

Most people don't feel a sense of responsibility for collective liberation, so stepping away is an option. By stepping away I don't mean organizing differently, I mean stepping away and fading either into assimilation or more despair, hating both the systems of oppression and our communities who *should* be doing better. Many end up hating our communities more than the systems of oppression that drive this culture.

It's hard to be in despair and show up everyday anyway, not everyone can do it. You have to be a special kind of broken for that, either needing to replicate victimhood and/or you've accepted responsibility for collective liberation and know how to care for yourself in the face of the violence. Regardless of why we are in liberation work, we can grow towards a liberatory culture that actually moves us towards a collectively liberated world.

We can not claim resistance when we do not understand our oppression — the oppression that we survive everyday and the oppression that is routed into our neural pathways in our mind. To assume we know how to be in liberated space together without rerouting our neural pathways and learning liberatory relationship and community building skills is dangerous.

Systems of oppression keep us so exhausted from surviving them that often we do not have the space to learn and move through liberation. It feels good to assume that our existence is resistance—that our existence is enough. But if it's not an investment in a future where we have the space to dismantle systems of oppression and build a liberated world then it's not actually enough. When we claim rest as resistance we must claim the additional space that rest provides for us to be revolutionary. When we claim joy as resistance we must claim that joy as fuel to remake the world. I want to honor that "rest as resistance" comes from Black organizing culture to address the lasting effects of slavery in the form of grind culture. That is not the "rest as resistance" I'm talking about here. I'm talking about the version of this idea that has been co-opted and watered down by non-Black folks.

There is a saying in Arabic that I learned at the precipice of the Syrian Revolution.

"الحرية لا تُمنح بل تُنتزع"

"Freedom is not granted, it is seized"

Liberation does not just happen to us. Liberation happens through resistance.

The culture of being broken impacts how and if we resist systems of oppression to build a liberated world. If we believe brokenness means we are always resisting then we fail to be active participants in building a liberated world — we don't seize our liberation.

When we claim brokenness as a way of claiming all that we are—and tapping into the humanity that exists beyond the brokenness—then we are able to begin seizing our liberation. That starts individually and collectively and in everything that we are.

Many will witness these words and feel exhausted, assuming that this is hard work. But being better broken is actually not that hard.

I am tired of everyone assuming everything is hard. Hard is subjective and hard isn't going away. You not having healthcare today doesn't become easier tomorrow. Access to water doesn't get easier if we do nothing. Standing on the sidelines as genocide ravishes the world is not easy.

You want to talk hard?

Let's talk about mass death. Let's talk about genocide. Let's talk about everything you and your people having ever known eaten by the ocean. Let's talk about volcano eruptions and earthquakes. Let's talk about fires. Let's talk about fascist regimes.

Everything gets harder the longer we wait.

In comparison, being better broken isn't that hard, resisting is the easier option. If it's between your house on fire or addressing a conflict which will it be? If it's between your children being forcibly sterilized or closing down an airport which will it be? I can go on and on, but if you don't get the point yet I don't think a list will do.

But I don't want you resisting because you fear what will happen to you. That's not a shared responsibility. That's not collectivism. That's not actually liberation. That's wanting a form of fascism that doesn't touch you. That doesn't make you better broken. That makes you a democrat.

Resist because someone you will never meet is going to be killed. Resist because islands thousands of miles away are being claimed by the ocean and millions are being displaced. Resist because if we do not build a better world genocide and famine will continue being our norm.

Don't even resist because you benefit from oppression, from the island sinking and genocide, even though you do.

Resist because this isn't about you at all. Resist because the world deserves liberation, not because fascism will come for you and not because you benefit from the fascism. Usually those last two are used as motivators to mobilize people. That can be strategic depending on what we're doing, but it's not a path for liberation and worldbuilding. The world builders resist because we stand for liberation unconditionally. We demand utopia always, regardless of our own circumstances.

The truth is, this isn't about any of us. It's so much more than anything we will ever be. Systems of oppression have taught us that resistance can be rooted in individualism, that liberation is exclusively about us as a single body. When we make liberation about us then we get lost in the space between assimilation and liberation, mistaking assimilation for resistance, while systems of oppression thrive.

Saying you going to a party is resistance is centering your ego. Saying you breathing is about resistance is centering yourself. These sayings are about our resistance as individuals but **we don't exist as individuals**.

My existence would be seen as resistance more than most. But it's not about me. If my visibility is resistance it is with purpose and strategy. If I go to a party as a form of resistance it is with purpose and strategy. The things I do directly contribute to liberation. I'm not perfect, I won't say 100% of everything I do is always about liberation. I just had a churro ice cream sandwich while writing this, the only liberation in the experience is writing these paragraphs; the intention was just "I want a churro ice cream sandwich".

Most people hear "liberation isn't about you" and they internalize that as me telling them not to enjoy life. I'm telling you the opposite. Life is enjoyable when we let go of what we are not and claim all that we are and the possibilities that exist within us. There is joy in resistance because we are meant to be resisting. A fascist state is not good enough for me.

I can only imagine what this churro ice cream sandwich would taste like in a liberated world.

If this work is about me then I stand alone in my resistance.

The more we make things about us the heavier the weight, the more immobilized we become, the more we feel disempowered. We are not meant to be liberated alone. We are powerful beings together. I can write a book in a weekend if I needed to and get it in stores in less than a month (look up *blood orange*). Every single one of us is incredible, and we all play a role in building a liberated world. Our resistance will look different, defined differently by our skill sets and the community's needs. This isn't about me and I do not define my role as an individual. I don't write and publish a book in a month because I want to, I do it as a form of resistance because it is needed. If I claim a role that centers me then I may not be resisting systems of oppression.

I know my power; claiming it requires knowing that liberation is actually not about me at all. It's past my ego.

The number one thing I hear in conflict within organizing space is that someone or everyone is making liberation about themselves, not about liberation.

There are many who assume that liberation is tied to them, and girl you're not that important, go back to your party for pride. Liberation isn't about you. Liberation isn't because you're at risk from a fascist government. Liberation isn't because you lost your house. Liberation isn't even because your people experienced genocide. Liberation is because it has always needed to be, it's that simple. You are not what will liberate us AND we won't be liberated without us. We resist, we demand and seize a liberated world but it is not about us as individuals.

None of that can make sense if you have not worked with your ego.

THERE IS NO 'I' WITHOUT LAND, SPIRIT, COMMUNITY

Be Ego Broken

When I meet someone for the first time I'm tempted to tell them every aspect of my pain to get them to understand who I am. I am tempted but temptation does not translate to action.

A part of the temptation can be spurred by my Cancer Moon which yearns for understanding. Another part can be from a childhood filled with trauma, carrying both the fear of being seen and the fear of being invisible.

There is a lot at play the moment I meet someone. Yet I do not lead with the pain unless it's strategic. I know that if you can't see me without knowing the details then you can not see me when you have the details. I am seen by spirit, loved ones, and so much more regardless of story sharing. As I've done work on myself I know that acceptance from people is frivolous.

I have learned along the way that I may not always be seen, and whether or not I am seen is irrelevant to showing up in the world.

I have learned to understand my ego, honor it, and know that it is not relevant.

This was definitely the hardest chapter to write because there is an abundance of things that we can cover and I'm not sure we would be able to cover them all even if this entire book exclusively covered our ego. It's also an area that has been studied for thousands of years and the majority of it (I wouldn't be able to know if all of it) recognizes that to reach enlightenment or self-actualization is to move past the ego.

I don't know of any sources that say the opposite, where they say, actually we should be self obsessed. Well, I suppose there's the "survival of the fittest" white men and their theories but I don't really think of them as scholars of any value to my work or the work of my communities—recognizing that we don't learn things from their "scholarship". Sure, their "scholarship" has fucked up the world, but most of us do not know their names. They are irrelevant as individuals; their only relevance is the world they built. It is also telling that the people who center individualism are the ones building systems of oppression.

The ego is human, it is a part of us. I don't want to go into neurobiology or concepts of evolution or the multitude of other places we can take this. Instead, I want to center what is relevant and matters in this specific moment in relation to being broken.

There are a lot of theories out there and a lot of research and tests and various other things studying our egos, there is plenty to engage with beyond this book.

What matters here is simple. If we view ourselves exclusively as individuals then we are not moving towards collectivism. If we do not move towards collectivism we will not move towards a collectively liberated world. It's pretty simple, in my head at least.

I share this because that is the goal: collective liberation. A pathway to collective liberation is collectivism. Where ego falls into that varies drastically across time, place, and definition.

In some schools of thought ego death is what achieves enlightenment, in others it is being one with the ego. If the ego is the I, the selfhood, then it is dependent on where we are geographically, as we are informed differently by culture and how we experience the world. It varies greatly across time, for a person's selfhood a thousand years ago is different from a person's selfhood today. A person's selfhood in Gaza is different than in Mexico and so on and so forth. All of it impacts us and our sense of self.

With that in mind it is interesting to try to claim theories of the ego across time and space when it is ever evolving in certain ways. For example, if we were to claim collectivism and build a collectively liberated world, what, then is the ego in that world compared with the ego that I might be carrying in 2025 under various threats of fascism, authoritarianism, and continued genocide? What is the ego in Xuycun compared with Oslo today, or even Xuycun compared with Lenape Hoking, particularly what's colonially known as New York City? What is the ego next year? Sure, the ego itself does not actually change, but our connection to ego and our interpretations of how we're in relationship to ego do.

In the midst of genocide, your "I" is different than within the confines of safe, stable housing. Recently, as I have been clearing and moving away from things not serving me well, wounds that I have long thought healed are demanding attention. Many of these wounds were healed living on streets or in my car, many were healed in unhealthy spaces and relationships. Now, in more stable housing and security than ever before, I am being asked what healing those wounds would look like today. Everything is different now. I am different, all of me is.

This is true for everyone, regardless of experiences, but often we make assumptions about others' experiences and how that impacts ego.

For example, there are a lot of assumptions that we make about people experiencing genocide. For some, it is that everyone is collectivist and takes care of one another. Or we believe that everyone will be out for themselves, unable or unwilling to care about anyone but themselves.

We make these same assumptions for many things. Recently, someone asked if they can connect someone to me to receive community care funds. I asked if they were an organizer (very loosely defined) and they said "no, they're experiencing X". X is a form of oppression. I replied with "everyone I support is also experiencing X and more are world builders". The assumption that marginalization makes it impossible to do any work that is moving us towards collective liberation is not true. The opposite is also not true: experiencing oppression does not mean that we're going to be working towards collective liberation.

I have worked with people during genocide who would give the thing their self desires most for the benefit of others (not always their lives, for life is not always the most desirable). I have also worked with people who will abandon their own family if it meant they could survive. There is no judgement in either of these scenarios and there are millions of other scenarios in the middle. None are mine to judge, neither are they yours to judge. None of us definitely know how we will show up in any scenario. I pray we don't have to learn who we are when we have already lost everything.

My point is that there is no single experience that dictates our actions and our interaction with our egos. The same experience moves some people towards God and others towards atheism. There is no universality in responses to experience. Smarter people study this their entire lives, barely moving the needle in understanding.

My understanding of the ego comes from Islam, Palestinian culture, disability, and transness. The first two are easy for many to understand, the last two might not seem as direct.

Islamic scholars during the Islamic Golden Age presented immense scholarship about the ego. Even prior to Islam, the concept of the *Nafs* was prevalent in the Arab world and expanded upon through Islam and the subsequent expansion on astronomy, medicine, architecture, and various other sciences. Even as a child, my Muslim community would talk to us about the different aspects of the ego, how the ego develops, and how we move towards wholeness.

Similarly, my Palestinian culture was influenced by the concept of the *Nafs*—and in particular as a multi-generation displaced Palestinian who grew up in severe poverty due to displacement—my ego was developed through a culture of survival. Within the culture I grew up in, community cared for one another and no one was disposable. Our ego develops differently when we know that we have a role to play in our community and we are not easily replaced. The ego also develops differently when the entire world tells you "you" are not wanted, constantly moments away from being deported, unsure to where.

Similarly, as a disabled person I am seen as "broken" by society. I receive this message through actual words and through the way every part of society is structured in a way that is not ideal for me to thrive in this body. Internalizing that my body and mind are broken meant I also internalized that my "I" is broken, my selfhood is broken. In the past, it was in this brokenness that I found myself trying to complete my selfhood in unhealthy ways.

Society tells us that through assimilation we could be whole again, and a lot of people believe that. But selfhood isn't incomplete due to disability, or any of the other identities that are marginalized and told that we are incomplete. We are perfect in all the ways, the defect is systems of oppression.

Transness is similar. My entire life I have been told that "I can't possibly know who I am", both as a child and as an adult, as if I am cosplaying to myself.

Growing up, not understanding the concept of gender felt like there was something missing. Like I could not be complete because the world told me to be something that I wasn't and I didn't know what else I could be. My sisters understood gender in a way that I did not—not in actual understanding, that we will be defined by genitalia forever—but rather that there were distinct genders and I was not like them. I was treated like I was broken my entire life.

Unfortunately, I am not alone. I still remember a trans teenager asking me during a session four or five years ago if "trans people are lovable?" If I really try to remember my childhood then I would remember this question being asked in my mind for most of my life. I don't know any trans people who did not have the same question.

It's not as if that question does not come up for me anymore. As I have grown into myself and my liberation work the question has shifted to ask "what is love in a white supremacist imperialist capitalist world?" I no longer yearn to be lovable or even human according to these systems. We are not lovable in accordance with systems of oppression—now I claim power and validation in that recognition.

A large part of that growth has been in claiming my brokenness. It is in that brokenness that I found myself and how to move past my ego.

An Islamic teaching I value is that within us exists an extension of the universe. To me, that means within us is a perfect being, it is what we accumulate within our lifetimes that moves us away from enlightenment unless we return to claim it.

If a part of us is perfect, and it's everything around us that is not, then is the ego the representation of our outside world yearning to claim that perfection? Is it not like a child striving to be perfect for their parents?

I'm not going to lie and pretend like I haven't yearned for love from those around me my entire life. Yearning is human, to love is to be human.

The ego is a place where our fractures catch the light. But here's the thing. I may yearn to be loved by those who should have loved me, but I will not compromise my being for that love. There is a difference.

As a child, my conditioning taught me to be desired, that if I was "better", those around me would love me. But love is not about worthiness. Those around me did love me despite the neglect that came from multiple jobs trying to survive capitalism. If I had been a better student my dad would still not have had time to spend with me because an A+ was not going to pay rent.

Time, attention, and desirability are not love.

My ego would love more attention, but it now knows that it is not lovelessness preventing me from feeling loved, it is oppression. Understanding oppression allows us to be in relationship with our ego in a way that allows us to focus on what matters most: building a collectively liberated world.

I can honor a yearning and know that I want to be held by revolutionary humans yearning for collective liberation like I am. My ego does not move me away from collective liberation. In fact, it maps the areas that we are able to build in utopia. Every yearning is a message, a call to action to build a better world.

In most of the spaces I have visibility into, that is not how we are moving with the ego. Instead, even in spaces yearning for liberation, so many are ego driven: Liberation is **not** about each of us as individuals, as mentioned in the previous chapter.

Yearnings are just that. Every emotion is a powerful driving force for action, but is also only an emotion. To get lost within emotions in ways that stop us from moving towards collective liberation is the problem. Believing that we are the only building blocks of collective liberation and that collective liberation serves us is harmful.

We are meant to be liberated, but liberation is not about us, it is not that we yearn for liberation and thus create it. Liberation is guaranteed, moving in ways that support this reality is not about us, it is about everyone and everything that has ever existed.

When we have not shed the conditioning of systemic oppression, the ego tells us that we matter above all else. When we have shed the conditioning of systemic oppression, the ego reminds us that we are part of a whole and there is no "I" without land, spirit, and community. We live and we die, liberation guaranteed in our lifetimes.

"Liberation in my lifetime" is not saying liberation will happen during this single body's lifetime, it is saying it is guaranteed in our collective lifetime.

We will be free, even if this body never lives in a free world.

WE DO NOT
HAVE TO
SOLVE
EVERYTHING

Be Generative Broken

I have had many jobs and have been in countless meetings—unfortunately most people have been in countless meetings. As an engineer, project management was a huge part of my role in the Fortune 500 that I unfortunately worked in. I do not waste any experience, so despite being within an evil corporation I also learned efficiency in a way that I did not find within organizing spaces and non-profits. Things got done.

Particularly in my role as a compliance and then quality engineer things needed to get done, well and fast. I didn't have the privilege to sit in meetings for the sake of being in a meeting that could have been an email. If I was in a meeting, I needed something specific and had to find ways to get it. If I didn't get it from a virtual meeting, I was going to go to someone's desk, even if they were in a different country. Things had to get done, and they did.

Most people despise useless meetings and yet still participate in them and don't realize that they are a part of the culture that birthed these meetings.

But it's not just meetings. It's phone calls, texts, reports, and so much more.

Within peer support and death work trainings I have led I have always done at least a full day to train about communication, recognizing that most people do not learn how to communicate with one another properly.

Now, I understand that properly is another word for **generative**.

The difference between effective and ineffective meetings is whether or not they are generative. Within business and engineering there are countless books about how to effectively communicate. Self-help also covers communication extensively. Yet, for some reason it does not feel that the message has been shared broadly across society, in particular within radical organizing spaces. Don't get me wrong, there are some organizing spaces that are incredibly effective, but for every one, there are at least 10 of a similar size that are not.

From my experience even a single effective communicator can create a generative space. On the flip side, a single person who is not generative can create spaces that never generate anything.

Being generative is a way of being, it is a practice, not a single action or another.

I am currently in a plane. There are a few things I can do in this place. I view all as generative. I can nap, read a book, write, listen to music, watch something or any combination—currently I'm listening to music and writing. Regardless of what I do it will be generative because I create the pathways to make it generative.

Take one of the things on that list that may sound not generative to you and think about how to make it generative. Napping allows me to rest. Reading allows me to rest. Writing allows me to rest. Music allows me to rest. Watching something allows me to rest. For some people some of these things are a waste of time, but in my practice I do not believe such a thing exists. Even if I stare at the seat in front of me doing absolutely nothing I am in a state of rest because I choose to be. You may assume that rest is wasteful, but for me, rest is a way of integrating learning and expanding my capacity. It is not the capitalist notion of self-care to be more productive later. Rest is about efficiency and effectiveness—rest is generative or it can be wasted.

I claim being generative always, nothing to be wasted. For another person presented with the same options they might find the opposite. It is not about the actions themselves necessarily, it is about how we claim them.

Recently I asked for a meeting with someone. This meeting was to discuss something very important. I offered times that worked for me. This was the response:

Those times do not work for me.

This is not a generative response from them but it is generative for me, because it tells me that they are not the person I need to meet with; it will not be wasted. This meeting was for this individual, they needed something from me, something very important. The only person negatively impacted by this meeting not happening is them, not the other way around. They failed to be generative in a way that would have supported them drastically. Instead, that was the response. There is no followup to that response.

A generative response could have started with the same line and followed with times that work for them or asking me to send other times that work.

Being generative is to have a followup, there is an AND at the end of the meeting or call or email or plane ride. I am writing and it is restful and after the rest...

Being generative is critical to navigating every interaction in our lives and more than that, it is not possible to have vision and strategy without having a generative practice.

Vision is what comes after AND. Strategy is how we achieve that vision.

Being generative impacts every aspect of organizing. Earlier I discussed the response to harm "well that individual is broken". That response is not generative in any way. There is no AND. In fact, not only is there no AND, we are actually moving backwards. We are doing the opposite of being generative. Going backwards creates more harm, we are breaking down the little bit of infrastructure we may have had. With that line alone I will no longer tell you when I am harmed. Our relationship (whatever it looked like) was also harmed in the process.

But nothing is wasted. In the process I now know where you stand, I see areas of improvement for our relationship, and I will reflect on if our relationship is strategic to maintain or if it's more strategic to step away from.

We can not be wasteful in our relationships and generative in liberation work at the same time. Being generative is a practice—something I learned through the practice of no waste.

I learned the concept of no waste theoretically in engineering school, but in practice, I learned it from my grandfather.

During my freshman year at an evil neoliberal institute, I took a class that was meant to be about understanding the greatest challenges of our time and how to solve them. Of course, the answer that we should dismantle the global north was not presented as a solution and all the solutions were neoliberal—however, a concept that we covered that I connected with is no waste, specifically the concept from cradle to grave. This concept was specific to manufacturing and the lifecycle of products. If you design a product within a no waste system then you are not wasting anything throughout the process. Beyond the one class this concept was then utilized within things like Lean Manufacturing and other Industrial Engineering practices. Generally, no waste in manufacturing means that everything that would have been qualified as waste within the process is then reused in a different way ensuring that we are not contributing to additional landfills throughout the manufacturing process or at the end of the product's lifecycle.

The same concept can apply to everything in life. Within capitalism it is extremely difficult to fully live a no waste life. However, we are able to move towards that as a goal in our lifetimes. No waste to me is not just about material creation, it is about everything: time, ideas, emotional investment.

In practice, I witnessed this with my grandfather. My grandfather taught me about compost before I knew there was a word for it. He reused water that was used in the house for his garden. No food was ever wasted: some was used to feed the stray cats and some as compost for his garden. Old clothes were repurposed. Everything was repurposed in one way or another. You would think he would have been celebrated by the rest of the family. But being not wasteful within an internally colonized family meant that the family offered little support and he was often met with violence from his children and their children—my immediate family being the only ones who were not harmful to him.

I was always a child who witnessed and then practiced, regardless of the consequences. College gave me language for what my people have always known and practiced.

Engineering has come up quite a bit and engineering is about solving problems. I want to be mindful to not send the message that being generative is to problem solve all the time. The AND is not always about solving problems. The AND can also be about sitting with problems.

As a yin yoga practitioner and practicing Muslim who prays 5 times a day I know that sitting in discomfort within a physical practice allows us to go deeper instead of always residing on the surface. Going deep and sitting with challenges and the realities around us allows us to better understand them. This allows us to reach a stronger standpoint to make decisions about the challenges. We do not have to solve everything. Not everything needs to be resolved. Many times the problem we see is not the actual problem.

When a friend comes to me with a problem I will always attempt to ask "What do you need in this moment?" Sometimes the answer is to brainstorm and try to solve the problem. Other times it's to vent and talk shit knowing that we're in a slice of reality where nothing exists within or outside it. Sometimes it's just to nod. Sometimes it's to be told they're right, sometimes it's that they're wrong.

When I approach someone with a problem I tell them what I desire at that moment. Usually, I know how to resolve things. Sometimes it's nice to not fix things at that moment. Sometimes it's nice to feel like the victim even when you know you're not.

Of course, I will not lie about reality either and those close to me and I know how to dance around that line. For example, if a friend comes to me and says that they were the victim when in fact they did something wrong, they know that I will tell them afterwards. They can play the victim for a little while but if they genuinely do not know that they are wrong, it is my responsibility to tell them. It is their responsibility to tell me when I am also messing up and assuming I am not. It is both our responsibility to own our lives in a way that when someone tells us we're wrong, it does not lead to violence. I want more relationships where we can tell one another (in these words): "you're fucking up".

There are many communication models that tell you we must find gentle ways for feedback for one another. "You're fucking up" is gentle in my opinion. Different relationships need different things, but I want us to move towards a world where we are responsible enough with ourselves and others that someone offering feedback the wrong way is still acceptable. Saying we always have to be gentle is saying that those harmed have to take responsibility for your reaction to being told you're wrong. This is not advocating for harassment and bullying one another. This is still about being generative.

When a friend tells me "you're fucking up", or I say it to a friend, either I or they will immediately follow it with "what happened?" or another generative question. I do not want to go around and tell people they're fucking up without a generative conversation. That means that I will tell them they are doing something wrong, what it is, and offer pathways for fixing it. I may not have the solution but I can brainstorm with them, I can sit with them as they figure it out, I can support them with additional pathways to make things right. The conversation does not end.

I am a person who critiques a lot—there is a lot to critique out there. AND I will always offer pathways. Even the groups I hate will always have an open pathway for us to move forward, but they have to participate. You can not have a one-sided generative relationship.

Currently, there are a lot of transphobic organizations. I will call them what they are—not everyone is happy with me doing so. AND I make it clear, I am willing to invest resources for them to do better and for us to be in generative relationship someday if it's strategic for collective liberation. Also, within my no waste practice I will still use their transphobia to move us towards collective liberation, specifically by accessing and redistributing resources to the most marginalized trans people. No waste.

Everything can be generative or can cause harm.

For some individuals and communities, critique is a way of preventing being generative. Different models exist but it's probably evident that I disagree with them. Shying away from what are considered difficult conversations ensures we never move towards our goals, meaning we are never generative. Again, this is not to say that we have to discuss and address everything, we do not, but it is about strategy and being clear about the world we're moving towards.

For example, in the fight for Palestinian liberation post Oct 7th 2023, many organizations (predominantly non-palestinian run) refused to center any trans Palestinian issues saying: "We don't want to lose our base". In a world where Palestinian and trans liberation are inherently tied, ignoring trans justice is not strategic. But these identities are intrinsically tied to the rise of fascism we are witnessing. Addressing this gap is strategic and necessary to achieve our goals.

The reality is that transphobic pro-Palestinians will never lead to a liberated Palestine. And similarly anti-Palestinian trans people will never lead to a world with trans justice. The same applies to anti-Blackness, anti-Indigeneity, ableism, queerphobia, anti-poverty, and all other forms of oppression. They are all intrinsically tied together.

We will never be able to dismantle white supremacy without dismantling capitalism. We can not dismantle capitalism without dismantling neo-liberalism or patriarchy. If we dismantle one without the others then we have just allowed it to evolve into something else, never actually resolving the problem. This is where sitting with things is necessary.

Without sitting with all the forms of oppression around us we might assume that only one is to blame, that parts of the systems of oppression are salvageable. None of it is salvageable.

I recently spoke to university students in a class about activism. A student group presented about environmental activism and discussed various ways the environmental crisis impacts folks globally and some pathways for activists to show up. As soon as I started speaking I made it clear: we will not fix the climate catastrophe if the global north and the systems that grant it authority over the world remain in existence. There is no collectively liberated world with imperialist empires stealing and hoarding resources and actively destroying the planet.

Be generative. Be strategic.

There are many things we can incorporate to move towards being generative and strategic.

Here are some tips that I normally provide during my trainings:

1. **Ask open ended questions that allow the conversation to flow.**

Open ended questions are questions that are not answered with a yes or no or one-word answer. Often they are questions that start with what, how, or why. Sometimes we may ask a yes or no question and receive a longer answer and for that we are grateful; but open ended questions open wider pathways for generative conversations.

2. **Repeat back what was said using the exact same words.**

It may appear that we're all using the same terminology and definitions, but we rarely are. **Ask for definitions.** It might be tempting to use words that you would use when repeating what you just heard; but without definitions we could be talking about very different things.

3. **Listen to understand, not to respond.**

In a world where we are constantly rushing we might be tempted to just want to get things over with, including getting our response in. We might assume we already know the information the other person has to share. This is not true, there is no level of experience that makes it so we know everything. We do not. Our role is to listen first and foremost. The response comes after.

4.   **Sit with the situation.**

Similar to above, we don't need to respond immediately even when someone asks for immediate advice. Unless the situation is dire and incredibly time sensitive we can respond at a later time or sit in silence together as we allow the situation to surround us.

5.   **Understand your role in the situation.**

We all play different roles in every situation. Every relationship is different. Knowing our role at specific times is critical to being generative. Being generative is not always offering opinions, thoughts, and solutions. Being generative can also be sitting with a person as they figure it out—allowing them to develop their own skills. Sometimes it's stepping away from a situation entirely. And sometimes we are responsible for protecting others and stepping in even when we are not wanted.

6.   **Hold hope for unlimited pathways forward.**

If I believe a situation is impossible when someone approaches me with a challenge they will feel my hopelessness. Instead I practice hope; I practice the generative mindset of "yet". None of us will ever know everything, and we're not meant to. Just because we haven't witnessed something doesn't make it impossible.

7. **Reflect on how you practiced being generative.**

Being generative is a practice, which also means that it is a muscle we grow over time. Sometimes we're more generative than others.

8. **Be accountable and grow.**

Acknowledge when we're actually not generative: We do not waste the times we are not generative. Instead we reflect on how it went and how it can be better next time and the time after and the time after that, until we're no longer here.

I am not always generative, no one is.

I have heard all kinds of excuses as to why people are not generative: brokenness, trauma, neurodivergence, disability, difficulty, and so much more.

Being generative is not about capitalist outcomes—even though that was the theory I was taught. Being generative is about moving forward. We are all capable of being generative. Capitalism dictates control over outcomes. Being generative is non-attachment in action, recognizing we don't control outcomes and are still able to move towards where we are meant to go.

When I work with intimate partners we always start with a conversation about non-attachment and how to be generative. This means we do not define the end goal in your typical couples counseling sense. I explain that the goal can not be that they must stay together or to resolve a specific challenge. Instead, it's about something beyond that, such as wellness or liberation. Sometimes the liberatory thing is to break up, other times it's getting married. I don't define these things and I work with partners—whether two or a group of seventeen—to move past surface level outcomes.

A generative meeting is not about a seventeen item list that comes out of it. Sometimes it's one thing, sometimes it's nothing.

We can all be generative. To truly be generative we do not abide by the capitalist definition of what generative is and looks like. We define it, we feel it, we live it no matter how broken. We are generative broken.

NONE OF US MATTER MORE THAN THE WORK

person. In most places, a single conflict can destroy the entire community. To me, that is a community that does not understand collectivism or the assignment at hand.

Within systems of oppression we are crafted to be individualistic, to assume that we matter more than anything else. That is false. I don't care who you are, how "good" you are, or anything else, you are irrelevant in the grander scheme of things. I am irrelevant in the grander scheme of things. I do not do this work to be relevant, I do this work because we are meant to be moving towards collective liberation always; always moving towards stewarding land and caring for one another.

Individual relationships can be building blocks to supporting this work, but at the end of the day there is no relationship that matters more than liberation.

So make it irrelevant.

Make conflict irrelevant.

Make miscommunication irrelevant.

Make your ego irrelevant.

Make your healing irrelevant.

When I say irrelevant, I don't mean we shouldn't strive for conflict transformation, better communication, working with ego, and healing. I mean that where we are on our journeys should not be what makes or breaks liberation work. Do all the work, but if doing the personal and interpersonal work comes at the cost of collective liberation or supporting the most marginalized of the most marginalized or stewarding land then what are we doing?

None of us are relevant enough to harm the work.

In so many ways this might seem like it is bordering on disposability culture. But y'all, what is the point of healing, better communication, conflict transformation or anything else if it's not in service to something greater? We do not exist for individual bliss. You can not be anti-systemic oppression AND want to uphold the narratives oppressors use to oppress us.

Moving towards healing, better communication, conflict transformation, working with ego, and various other things are meant to move us closer towards our purpose of building a collectively liberated world. They are meant to aid us on this journey, not pre-emptively end the journey.

When I train individuals in these modalities we always start with making our own journeys as irrelevant as possible. Particularly, I am often asked about how we move through conflict and my response is to make it irrelevant. I can and do offer multi-day moving-through-conflict training to understand how to resolve and transform conflict. I conduct months-long transformative justice processes and practice building with communities worldwide, but they are built on a foundation of finding ways to make conflict irrelevant. Again, that means that no conflict supersedes the work. Liberation work comes first.

At a recent event in Lenape Hoking, I mentioned that I have not seen many conflicts being resolved in spaces. A loved one at the event reminded me that there was a conflict between them and another loved one that was, in fact, resolved. I loved that I was reminded of this incident and I used it as an example at that event. This conflict was between two individuals co-facilitating a long term program together. The program was commissioned by me and I was notified of what happened by the individuals separately. Here's why and how this conflict was resolved.

The first critical thing was that both individuals prioritized the program above their own individual experience of the situation. There was never a concern for if and how this conflict would negatively impact the community at large: i.e. it was irrelevant.

I had individual conversations. I am trained in conflict transformation. One of the two is a conflict expert, the other is partially trained.

The two individuals chose to pursue resolution for a possible long-term relationship beyond the program. Within a couple of conversations, they were able to resolve and grow. Mediation by me was offered but it was not needed.

This conflict wasn't smaller than other conflicts that have torn entire communities apart and destabilized liberation work.

When we prioritize the work and we know how to move through conflict we are able to move together. Who knew?

When we prioritize liberation, everything else becomes irrelevant momentarily and then everything becomes useful to making the work more effective and efficient. With this philosophy the work is never harmed and it is always positively impacted. It is the opposite in the majority of spaces currently. This is a culture we get to shift.

I am often asked about the step by step guide of moving through conflict, communication, healing, and whatever else. I always say to start with a healthy foundation. If you start with a foundation that prioritizes collective liberation, everything else follows. If you start with action without a foundation, then sooner or later you will free fall.

Building a healthy foundation is something that happens in tandem to the work, but action without foundation is never sustainable. A foundation without action is also inadequate.

Build a foundation on collectivism, responsibility for collective liberation, no waste, being purpose driven, stewarding land and caring for one another, and body-mind-spirit balance.

No Waste

When I normally talk about foundation building I don't include no waste as a philosophy. However, as I lead more trainings to support groups in understanding strategy, I am realizing how needed a no waste philosophy is. Strategy is developed through wisdom.

No waste is a beautiful practice to develop wisdom over time and is a strategic philosophy.

Once I learned no waste in the world of engineering, I began incorporating it into my mental health work immediately (without really knowing that I had).

In my mental health world no waste became a philosophy that centered the idea that all of our experiences, whether good or bad, are valuable. I realized years later that this is the same concept that I have lived my entire life through Palestinian and Islamic practices.

In my organizing world no waste is about strategically utilizing the things that you would not perceive as helpful in a helpful way for the work you are doing. For example: it may seem that being doxed is exclusively bad. It is bad, AND it can be utilized to convince funders that additional money is needed for the community.

A march that upholds transphobia even as it demands liberation sounds harmful but is also a pathway for community building, accessing resources, and solidifying trans justice work. This is no waste.

No waste helps develop wisdom, but without the wisdom of a body-mind-spirit balance it is more challenging to find the space to practice the philosophy of no waste.

Body-Mind-Spirit

We often invest in our minds. We go to workshops, read self-help books, even reading my books is an investment in our minds. Our minds do not exist in a silo. Our journeys do not occur in a single layer of our being, it must happen in balance.

In many spiritual practices you will learn that to achieve higher mental and spiritual access you must train your body. This is why most spiritual practices have a physical practice component. Many religions have physical prayer, in the form of salat, asanas, or countless others. These physical practices are what allow us to achieve higher levels of consciousness and spiritual connection.

Being better broken requires physical practice as much as it requires any other liberation framework. I like to think about this work in the following way.

Within all of us exists a cup that is filled to the brim with systemic oppressive conditioning. If you try to add a liberatory practice the cup overflows and it is not retained. To be able to incorporate a practice into our being we must make space for it by removing some of the liquid in the cup. OR, we increase the size of our cups (yes, that's a thing!!). Physical practice allows us to expand the size of our container, allowing us to expand our limits in how we hold, witness, and process.

You can do the deconditioning work—you should do the deconditioning work. But ultimately if your capacity to hold is always a small cup's worth of liberation then that is your limit, but if you do both the deconditioning and the expanding your capacity work then you are limitless.

The body is the step before starting. Then we start. We invest in our minds, and ultimately we reach higher levels of spiritual consciousness. Higher levels of spiritual consciousness is what allows us to truly reach and embody collectivism.

Collectivism

I write extensively about collectivism in *whispers beneath the orange grove* and *living to 99: collectivism, non-attachment, liberation*. Put simply (but please read those other works to best understand this topic) collectivism is how everything is connected: human, land, spirit, and everything within those. Collectivism is not about "our people", collectivism is a connection beyond individuals and groups of people, creating a broader ecosystem where we are of and one with the universe. This is not likeability politics, this isn't about me or you or everyone you call "family", this is everything connected—even those we don't like.

Without collectivism, we limit stewarding the land and caring for one other.

Stewarding Land and Caring for One Another

I also write extensively about this topic in *living to 99: collectivism, non-attachment, liberation* and to a lesser degree in *whispers beneath the orange grove*. In *whispers beneath the orange grove* I start the book with an essay about being a settler on stolen land, followed by an essay about collectivism. There is no stewarding the land without connection to land, there is no connection when we are not mindful of our positionality on land. Our connection with land is critical to collectivism, and without collectivism caring for one another would be incomplete because it never moves beyond the individual.

Collectivism is the thread that connects us to both land and others and enables us to fulfil our purpose of stewarding land and caring for one another.

To steward is to care for something entrusted to you. To care for the land is a practice. To care for others is a practice. To accept this assignment is to accept responsibility for collective liberation.

Responsibility for Collective Liberation

The second half of this book is entirely about responsibility for collective liberation. It asks what it would actually mean to be responsible for liberation. The thing with responsibility is that it is a practice over a lifetime, it is not something that changes with ease.

When we claim responsibility for land, responsibility for caring for others, and for collective liberation,, we dedicate everything that we are to the work and we do not move away from it with ease. Most people yearning for liberation do not feel a sense of responsibility for building a collectively liberated world. Many feel the injustice of having to do this work profoundly and expect and demand that someone else do it, that someone else needs to save us. But two things can be true at the same time. It is injustice that leads us to have to do this level of labor AND we are the only ones who can and will do it, no one is coming to save us, least of all the conscience of our oppressors.

When we do not claim the responsibility that we play a role in liberation work, then we prop up one or a few individuals as the leaders who will save us. We grant them pseudo-celebrity status and expect them to do the work, to strategize, mobilize, create art, mediate conflict—everything but mess up. Then they mess up, and we say "see, this is impossible, even they messed up", as if growth isn't a lifelong journey. As if we are not all responsible and accountable for this work.

It should go without saying that some of the "mess up" is large scale. Unfortunately, not everyone is in this work with the right intentions and want that kind of idolization. At the same time, there are many who do not want to be idolized in this way, who will actively resist, and are still canceled and used to avoid responsibility.

Some people might claim that I only share this because of my visibility, but I have been saying it for years, and at the end of the day I'm okay with being put on a pedestal. But for me, we are all to be placed on pedestals and have high expectations placed on us, the highest one being accountability. As I write that line I also want to claim the highest, highest expectation: responsibility for collective liberation.

In Conclusion,

I don't normally conclude a single essay, but I felt drawn to this one.

Here's the reality of the spaces we are in.

Many want to be mobilized.

Many claim to organize.

Very few want to claim responsibility for who they are, the work we need to do, and for collective liberation largely.

I have been asked by the same people again and again "what do I do?"

I have created many access points for folks to access my knowledge and wisdom. Many ask after engaging (reading books and coming to intensives), most ask before, and again and again as if there is an answer I can provide that will give them the thing they're searching for. They ask again and again because they are not satisfied that there is no single answer that will remake the world. There is no one easy solution or path to build a liberated world—I wish there were.

The thing standing in the way of collective liberation is not systemic oppression exclusively, it's that we wouldn't know how to live in a liberated world. We must learn how to live in a collectively liberated world to build it.

Learning to live in a collectively liberated world requires deconditioning from oppressive systems through practice, skill building to access that practice and to understand the deconditioning. This will not be achieved with a few minutes of Instagram videos, it can only happen through intensive training that allows us to build liberatory practice as we understand the theory. However, very few communities and individuals are willing and able to invest in long term liberation work.

I have been doing this work since the early 2010s. Between 2015 and 2023 I was doing roughly 80 hours of intensive training per community I worked with.

In the two years since Oct 7th, 2023, I have not done a single training more than 4 hours. My trainings are more accessible than they've ever been, offering $20,000 worth of training for free. Every community I go to wants the intensive training—none have done the work to organize the intensive training.

We know what to do. Black women told us what to do decades (if not centuries) ago. Do not ask what to do, ask why you refuse to listen when you are told.

Read and re-read these words. This work doesn't happen all at once, this is just one piece. But every piece brings you closer to knowing what to do by being receptive to it.

Be better broken. The work continues and it's never about us. Be better broken.

TO BE HUMAN IS TO BE AN EXTENSION OF THE UNIVERSE

To Be In Service

I assume that you have been called. Have you not?

The little call that you get at 3 a.m. or over lunch or a meal, on a date, or playing some kind of sport, or beginning to crawl and then walk, or at work, or as you're diagnosed with a terminal illness, or as you're getting fitted for your first wheelchair or at any time of any day at any point in your life before or maybe even during this moment. The little call that demands your service.

Perhaps a call that you have ignored until your Saturn return and all of a sudden you are here; or whatever else needed to happen to move you towards—at the very least—curiosity about what it would look like to be in service. That call. Have you received it?

The call that tells you **you are meant for more, you get to serve a purpose**. A call that demands for you to matter—not just a reminder that you matter.

If not, you are welcome to continue on this journey through this book, with an invitation to return to these words after receiving the call.

I do not control how or when you or anyone else will be called into service, just like I did not control my own calling; what you do beyond this moment is always yours.

If you have been called, welcome. I have no idea what any of these words or holding this book will do for you.

What you do beyond this moment is always yours. Always.

****

In a lot of ways—basically all of them but I'm told I generalize a lot so I'm using my generalizations sparingly—I believe we all have purpose; every human and everything beyond what is human has callings. I like to frame callings as "being in service".

When you look at definitions of service there are countless definitions that center being helpful and contributing to someone or something's welfare. At the same time, it can mean servitude or even being a servant. Servitude and being a servant have a negative connotation within many of our societies—and for good reason considering the history of the slave trade, current enslavement practices through capitalism and incarceration, and various other forms of oppression that continue to enslave the most marginalized of the most marginalized.

Capitalism and other oppressive systems that predate it have told us for hundreds of years that to be in service is to be weak, to be denied autonomy, to be taken advantage of. We are taken advantage of every single day—and also being in service is a beautiful thing that has been weaponized against us.

I use the words *in service* to claim the beauty of a concept so natural and liberating that, like so many other concepts, has been weaponized. Reclaiming liberatory concepts and practices allows us to expand the areas of our work. Without reclaiming liberation we risk moving to another extreme, something I witness often. When service is always seen as negative then the assumption becomes that to be anti-capitalist means to not be *in service* at all. But there is no collective liberation without service to the collective. If none of us contribute to community then there is no community—there is no liberation.

Service is neither positive nor negative, it just is—whether we deny it or not, it is always occurring. When we do not know what we are *in service* to we maintain the service we are conditioned into—often, service to uplift and maintain systems of oppression instead of liberation.

Being in service that honors our humanity means a dedication to a purpose coming from a place of deep relationship with land, spirit, humanity, and all the things that words can't easily capture. I believe humans are capable of the entire spectrum of violence and liberation, we choose violence. However, I also believe that there is a yearning within all of us to move towards liberation—to be in service in ways that move us towards liberation. When we are *in service* to fascism and oppression we are not in balance and harmony with all other creation around us. We are in balance when we are in service that honors our humanity.

I am in service. I have always been in service.

Being in service is not something that is always easily named and it is not in exchange for gratitude and acknowledgement. It is nice to be acknowledged, it is nice not to be erased, but more importantly it's nice to be in service regardless.

We are always *in service* to something whether we know it or not. I have spent decades (even before formally organizing) asking those around me what they are *in service* to. Growing up the answer was always *in service* to Spirit, Allah, The Divine. Some defined that service in liberation and justice work, while others defined it in dogmatic prayer and reading the Quran. I will not hide my animosity towards the latter. The study of anything without any liberatory action is not a form of service that I appreciate, especially in these times. I feel the same whether that's within religion, academia, art, or any other sphere where the purpose is not to act. I say this as someone who practices Islam daily, has a masters degree and has a few toes in academia, and as an artist. All those things are part of being *in service* to liberation for me. We are always *in service* to something.

I have had many roles throughout my life and I have always been *in service* to liberation.

Being able to name who or what we are *in service* to or *for* is essential for recognizing our power, understanding the roles we play, and for world-building—to name just a few things.

Initially, I wanted to start with being *in service* to a Revolution, but my service extends beyond The

Revolution, and I'm talking about *The* Revolution—the one that actually dismantles the systems we currently know today. I'm not here to talk about hypotheticals: in my mind The Revolution and The World post The Revolution are guaranteed and I am invested in that world.

For too many years I had desired for my service to end at The Revolution or some years in the lead up to it. I have asked myself often what my ultimate *in service* is, what it is all founded on. For me, it is similar to those around me in my childhood, I am *in service* to Spirit and that means I am *in service* in this lifetime to stewarding land and to all creation. Being *in service* to Spirit does not end because things get difficult, it does not even end in this lifetime. My life may end at any time but I will always be *in service*. Whatever I am meant to become once this body is returned to the land will still be *in service*.

Identifying what you're in service to can tell you a lot about who you are and the world around you. For example, years ago, in my teens and early twenties I used to believe that being *in service* to Spirit is the same as being *in service* to my immediate family, particularly my sisters. I did not have enough of a grasp on understanding patriarchy to know that family is a way to weaponize our inherent desire for collectivism while moving us towards individualism. Caring for family alone is individualism. Being *in service* to family alone without greater service is being *in service* to patriarchy—most of us do not know this and many do not care.

We are all learning how to refine our service. That's what life is about. Life is about growing and growing and growing, moving towards efficiency, moving towards mastery. There are limitless entry points, limitless places we are at right now, and limitless pathways towards mastery—towards service to building and maintaining a collectively liberated world.

I wonder often—what is the point of anything if it starts and ends with a single person? Why would I heal myself if that healing is not moving me to mastery of being *in service?* Why build skill sets and understanding if they do not move us towards liberation?

I write these last few chapters six months after the rest of this book was written. I'm in what's known as Salt Lake City. The mountains hover to my left, as if embracing me like I embrace them. I have just returned from a trip to the desert, where the mountains are so loud I can't tell their voices apart from my own thoughts. I am *in service.* The mountains are *in service.* In the exact middle of this view, between me and the mountains is a giant american flag waving with the light mid-morning wind—a reminder that our service (mine and the mountains') intersects in ending this empire.

We are always in service: When we do not claim liberatory service then we are usually upholding systems of oppression with our service—often, we are doing both at the same time. Our goal is to move towards one end intentionally while limiting what we do for the other in the meantime.

How, when, where, who, all matter in how we understand and claim service. We are *in service* always. Without understanding how and when and where and who, we are always harming someone in the process. We are always harming someone within an oppressive world, the difference is strategy and it's making amends as we build a world where we are able to truly only be *in service* to stewarding land and caring for one another.

WE DO NOT EXIST FOR INDIVIDUAL BLISS

In Service to Liberation

Organizing work isn't about any of us as individuals and I will not do the one thing that will lead to collective liberation; I just show up in the ways I need to but ultimately, there will be an action—a final action built on millions of others that will lead to collective liberation. What if that's you? What would you change about your life and how you show up for liberation? What would your service to liberation look like?

If knowing that you will be the "one" changes your liberatory practice, then you have an ego attachment to liberation. If knowing that you will be the "one" changes how you show up, then you have an individualistic attachment to liberation.

I feel this thought exercise is a great gauge to check in about your levels of collectivism, individualism, and your ego. While not ideal, perhaps an ego attachment is what we need to begin. Many people are inspired for the wrong reasons, it doesn't mean that the labor and vision are irrelevant.

A reminder that we all have immense deconditioning work to do on our journeys; finding the things that are going to move us towards pathways for deconditioning is critical.

Within global north society we are all conditioned to be individualistic. Even within the global south, many societies have transitioned deeper into individualist societies through global north acculturation, even when they still claim to be collectivist.

So how would you show up if you knew you were the "one"? And maybe you're already showing up that way. If you are, then you're already *in service* to liberation—or you assume that you are.

Individualism tells us that our main priority within liberation work should be being "good" people. How we are seen and how we feel is what matters, the work itself is secondary (or lower on our priority list). Being *in service* to liberation is not about being a "good" person. Being *in service* to being a "good" person is going to lead us to extinction. This work isn't about us as individuals—it can't be. Being *in service* to liberation isn't about if I feel like I am fulfilling a purpose or need—that can be a part of it but it is not the entire thing. Liberation is a real thing, it is not defined by each individual; it requires specific skill sets and labor to be achieved. To say otherwise is to deny that our ancestors have been building liberatory practices longer than oppression has existed.

I often hear individuals say that people in their lives are showing up for Falasteen and when I ask for examples they say that someone has fundraised, or shared about genocide on social media, or showed up to a protest. Rarely do I receive an answer that actually fulfills the assignment. This is not to say that digital campaigns, fundraising, and protesting are not a part of being *in service* to liberation. This is to say that we must be strategic, our *service* is dependent on various factors—our positionality, our skill sets, our vision. Too many people do the least assuming they are *in service* to liberation, assuming that any participation is enough and makes us "good" people. Fuck your sense of "goodness" or "righteousness" or anything else. Again, that is what individualism tells us liberation is. What matters is the work.

If you do not want to be *in service* to liberation then you have chosen where you stand. If you claim to be *in service* to liberation then that means something and requires labor and skill building to embody the work in strategic and effective ways.

Positionality

In the last decade I have conducted dozens of trainings on understanding and claiming power and roles within our lives. It is difficult—I won't say impossible—to understand service without understanding our positionality, which means understanding our power and our roles. In a world where there are barriers and consequences to liberation, then an understanding of the systems impeding our liberation is critical—this includes understanding where we fit into these systems and our role in dismantling them and building a liberated world.

Without understanding my positioning in these systems, in society, and more broadly in the world, then I can not understand my role, and if I do not understand my role how would I be able to fulfill it? This isn't to say that if you do not claim a specific role (can be incredibly broad and changes over time) that you can not be *in service* to anything. You can and you are *in service* always—the question is to what or who?

129

Understanding positionality allows us to begin honing in on our desire to be *in service* to liberation, not to the systems that supposedly uplift us and grant us "power".

True power is not dependent on systems of oppression, it is inherent. Humans have always been and will always be powerful. Systems of oppression maintain a specific form of power over other things through the theft of land and resources and through oppressing others. This power is temporary. In a liberated world we will return to true power. In a systemically oppressive world we are still inherently powerful—despite systems of oppression telling us otherwise. Every human carries both types of power. Power due to systemic oppression is constantly in flux based on our own and others' oppression. Inherent power does not fluctuate, however, we are able to move towards it as we decondition from systems of oppression and move towards liberatory practice.

We are powerful beings. Period. Understanding and claiming power is necessary to truly claim service to liberation. Once we understand our power then we can truly understand our roles.

If I do not know that I have power as a holder of a "u.s." passport then I will not know how to weaponize the passport globally to move us towards liberation. If I do not know that I am inherently powerful as a human then how will I know that to be kind is powerful and is a building block for care work, non-violent and violent resistance? How would I know that to be *in service* is human and to be *in service* is powerful?

Understanding power requires an understanding of how power changes like the weather, one room can be warm while another is cold—my wardrobe shifts accordingly and similarly my role changes in the world. In a room where I am the most marginalized I show up very differently than a room where I am the most privileged—and yes, there are spaces where I am the most marginalized and spaces where I am the most privileged. These days I am often the most powerful person in the rooms I walk into—my role has shifted over the years as I have understood and claimed power. Understanding my role has allowed me to move past powerlessness, imposter syndrome, and survivor's guilt. It's easy to look at the world and wonder why I have the life that I do and to spiral into oblivion and inaction; claiming roles moves us away from that. I have not "earned" my privilege, no one has—we have a responsibility to build a liberated world using every ounce of power we have access to, power that, in many cases, more marginalized folks do not have access to because we do.

My role is to be *in service* to liberation. I map out this journey as I do the work to build a liberated world every day. I understand, claim, and utilize every source of power I have for this role.

Skill sets

We are born with different skill sets—why and how depends on your belief systems and spirituality, and if you don't believe this that's okay. What's important to know is that from the day we are born we are sculpted to assimilate into systems of oppression, moving towards the oppressive class and as far from the margins as we can. This isn't conscious, this is a gravitational pull from everything around us, a pull that our parents, grandparents, and various others have been contending with their entire lives. By the time we are born they are already *in service* to settler colonialism, patriarchy, white supremacy, imperialism, capitalism and various other systems that currently exist around us. Conditioning is not optional, the only way to fully opt out is to not participate in any aspect of society entirely—if you're in society, you are conditioned to assimilate into these systems. The skills we develop over time are based on these systems. Our skills move us towards assimilation—one way or another. Even our skills to survive are about assimilation.

The thing with skills is that they are transferable.

Systems of oppression tell us that our skills are not transferable, that skills are "good" or "bad" and we assume that they must be entirely thrown out during the deconditioning process. In every strategy skill building session I've done I've had at least three people say that they thought strategy was "bad". For example, masking is something many of us have had to do to survive in a world that punishes us for our neurodivergence, disability, dark skin, gender, and so many other things. Masking has saved many of our lives. Masking who we are, code switching—whatever you want to call it—allows many of us to navigate

spaces with the least amount of harm possible.
Masking is about assimilation. Masking is also a skill set
I can use in this work, it's a skill set I use every day
intentionally and deliberately as I work to build a world
where masking is not necessary. Using it is a strategy.

Masking allows me to be an excellent resource
redistributor.

Masking allows me to be an excellent culture worker.

Masking allows me to move through what would be
considered difficult spaces.

Masking allows me to infiltrate.

This is not to say that skills learned through systemic
oppression should be the primary skills we use for
liberation. I am saying not to waste skill sets.
Understand and claim the skills you already have—and
develop new ones needed to move us forward, nothing
is to be wasted.

But we do need new skills: some that evolve from other
skills as well as completely new ones. As an engineer,
most of my education was about solving problems in
the most capitalist ways possible. Sometimes, the
same skill set is used both for profit and for
sustainability. For example, take the concept of "cradle
to grave", a concept that looks at manufacturing waste
and aims to reduce it—both for saving money and for
sustainability. That same skill set, and the philosophy,
can be used for different purposes, some assimilatory
and some that can be utilized to disrupt systems of
oppression.

Cradle to grave is a concept that I connected with due to the no waste concepts I grew up with in a displaced family living in severe poverty. And then I witnessed it in action with my grandfather's gardening, something he had done seventy years prior in Falasteen.

How we utilize our skill sets matter.

Some skill sets, such as knowing how to de-escalate a situation is something many of us learned as children around violent parents or adults. Many of us know how to work with individuals who manipulate and twist the truth for the same reason. All these are essential skill sets.

The skill sets we don't have are the ones that allow us to build liberatory worlds. We are taught to envision dystopia; a slight modification allows us to envision utopia. However, building that space rooted in kindness and accountability—that's newer for the majority of us.

If we are to be *in service* to liberation we must understand, claim, and utilize skills to build a liberatory world. I say liberatory instead of liberated because it is meant to continuously liberate us.

Far too many assume that we all know how to build a liberated world by virtue of being "good" people. If that were the case we would not be here. Very few know how to build a liberated world, many are thrown into this work modeling it after other organizers who came before them. Many of us learn unhealthy ways of moving through this work. We are not *in service* to liberation when we non-strategically martyr ourselves—both our bodies and our minds.

Being strategic is a skill set. Knowing which skills to use when and where is a skill set. Knowing how to maintain balance in this work is a skill set. Knowing how to sustain this work is a skill set. Martyrdom is also a skill set. Non-violence is a skill set. Violence is a skill set.

We develop skills through training, through lived experience, and through witnessing. I became the organizer I am through witnessing organizing as a child, through lived experience, and through literature reviews and training. Reading bell hooks, Audre Lorde, June Jordan, and others was transformational in understanding what I had witnessed growing up and into my adulthood. I was trained in peer support, death and birth, trauma support, engineering, yoga, body work, leadership, management, crisis coordination, and various other modalities that I incorporate into my organizing every day.

I have also learned how to be a better organizer by witnessing "bad" or unhealthy organizing. I have seen people die for this work in non-strategic ways, and I refuse to continue those legacies left behind by loved ones.

The last area I learned from is the intersection between my lived experience and witnessing: through harm directed at me by those who are *in service* to fascism. I have learned from every big death threat, doxxing campaign, and everything in between. My autistic brain has made me an expert on pattern recognition and understanding behaviors. I can learn just as much from enemies as I do from comrades.

Training is critical for individuals whose backgrounds are not at the margins of marginalization. When your lived experience is primarily one of privilege there is a high likelihood that you have lived a life segregated from the most marginalized and the larger harms of systemic oppression. You most likely have not witnessed the true power of organizing within a community and your lived experience has not forced you to develop skill sets for survival and to move past systems of oppression. Training in this case is almost always necessary.

Most individuals I know are never trained and instead learn through the work itself. After some experience doing the work most believe that they no longer need training because they have already been doing the work. There is so much beauty in learning within community, but there is no guarantee that what we're learning is truly liberatory work that moves us towards collective liberation. Often, we are taught what others know, but that does not mean that it's the most efficient and effective form of liberation work. As a result, almost everyone I know who has never been properly trained does not have a healthy foundation for their service, find great difficulty in moving through conflict and other challenges that will always occur, and rarely consider the culture of liberation necessary to move us forward. As discussed in the earlier chapters of this book, this often leads to harm within our communities and moves us away from liberation.

At the same time, you have some individuals who are uncomfortable doing the liberation work and would rather spend years trying to "figure something out" due to this discomfort. They may or may not seek training to help them figure "it" out. Once we have the skills we no longer have any excuses to not do the work. If I believe I do not have the skills to shut down a bridge then I can hide behind that, but if I am trained in shutting down bridges then I have no excuses not to when it is strategic to do so.

This came up at the start of the COVID-19 pandemic. As someone who had been organizing and running virtual spaces for five years at that point, the shift to virtual was seamless. At the time, I offered various organizations and groups support in moving their work virtually. None accepted, instead opting to shut down services for 6-9 months until they figured it out on their own.

Skill building has always been a part of our legacy as movement builders, but these days there are fewer and fewer places that will train you to be an organizer. The tens of thousands of individuals I've interacted with in the two years since Oct 7th, 2023 recognize they need training, yet very few are willing to commit to being trained, often citing capacity as a concern. Capacity is a concern AND capacity is a concern because we do not know how to effectively and efficiently organize and mobilize. I know from experience that eventually things are bad enough where either individuals leave the movement or get trained. I would love to see us seek and claim training before this point, but that is not something I control.

Our commitment to being *in service* to liberation must allow us to move beyond our ego, beyond our discomfort and terror of the work. It is our responsibility to gain and utilize the skill sets needed for our service. There is no other way.

Vision

I spoke with a front line organizer earlier today whose body is fully shutting down as a consequence of ten years of organizing in a way that did not take health, community and state violence, and so much more into account. They were saying that there has been something missing from their organizing and it is literally killing them. They are one of the best organizers I know in terms of people who can get things done, literally influencing tens of millions of people and entire regions in their organizing. Yet, they have never done the vision building work of what is to come beyond dismantling systems of oppression and, more importantly, the necessary work to live a liberated world on our way to creating it.

Many organize to prevent injustice. Some organize due to fear of what is to come for them and their families. Some organize for a vision of liberation. Some organize because building a liberated world is human. People organize for all kinds of different reasons. Our motivation for organizing impacts the types of service we are in and the methodologies that we utilize in organizing.

At times, individuals think that the vision building work I do is because I know what a liberated world actually looks like. I don't—and I love that I don't. I've never lived in a liberated world, nor has anyone I know, and what I can imagine is so limited compared to the possibilities I am yet to grow into.

Vision building is a practice of rerouting our neural pathways to move us away from dystopic thinking. This practice allows us to witness and embrace endless possibilities instead of just dead ends for the things happening in our lives—and it increases our capacity to witness and hold the realities of the world as it currently is and what it can be as we move towards liberation. Vision is meant to change how we live our lives, allowing us to live liberation before the systems we are working to dismantle are gone. Liberation exists always, even in a world where systems of oppression govern every part of our lives. Systems of oppression create barriers and consequences to liberation but they can not possibly eliminate it.

When we organize as liberated beings then we are able to create pathways for our service to be sustainable and not harmful to our bodies, minds, spirits, communities, and the planet. Living a liberated life is not one free of consequence, but I would argue that living in an oppressive world carries more consequences.

****

Earlier, I asked if your service would change knowing you would lead us to a liberated world. The same question could be asked about hope. If you knew for certain a collectively liberated world would happen, how would you show up today? There are countless questions that we may ask ourselves to gauge where we are and where we might be heading.

Recently, while speaking to students at a university in Kentucky, a student had sent in a question prior to my session that I adored, yet did not have time to answer: "if you don't want liberation, how do you still support others who do?" I can make assumptions about who this student is but I love the question.

We assume everyone is *in service* to liberation, or at the very least that everyone desires liberation. But that's simply not true. We are all conditioned to move away from liberation by systems of oppression. It is also simply not true that everyone will benefit from liberation and that everyone will be harmed by fascism. The vast majority of people who are beyond the margins of marginalization will benefit either way.

There are those who will suffer due to fascism. There are those *in service* to liberation. They are not the same group but they are not by any means mutually exclusive. You can suffer due to fascism and be *in service* to liberation. You can benefit from fascism and be *in service* to liberation. You can suffer due to fascism and not be *in service to* liberation. You can benefit from fascism and not be *in service* to liberation.

To assume that everyone who benefits from fascism will not be *in service* to liberation and everyone who suffers will be, we make a dangerous assumption about both groups. The truth is that everyone can be *in service* to liberation. The difference is that those of us who suffer due to fascism must be *in service* to survival and those who benefit are more deeply ingrained into systems of oppression and must claw their way out.

There are hundreds of books that talk about privilege and the different roles of those who benefit from the systems of oppression most compared to those who suffer the most, so I won't explore that much. What I am concerned with today is who is *in service* to liberation. There is no one identity that is always *in service* compared to others. In fact, I would argue that there isn't a single entire group of people that is *in service* to liberation, if there were, we would live in a different world.

Not all trans Palestinians are *in service* to trans and/or Palestinian liberation—assuming that we are all *in service* as marginalized individuals is dangerous and often leads to immense community harm.

Most of us would like to think that our families and friends are all "good" people, and are thus *in service* to liberation. Most of us want to believe that we ourselves are *in service* to liberation. Neither is inherently true.

I don't know what others' experience with this is like, if it's shocking, disheartening, or anything else when they discover that the people closest to them are not in fact invested in liberation. My autism allows me to recognize patterns fairly quickly, something that aids me in understanding roles and responsibilities, often better than the individuals involved themselves. However, there have been a few instances where I assumed that certain individuals were *in service* to liberation who ended up causing harm and then refused to recognize the harm and move towards accountability. Those instances hurt, and moved me towards reflecting on my ability to gauge people's sense of responsibility. I have wondered why others who are invested in my liberation are not invested in collective liberation. And I know that I do not control whether or not individuals move towards any kind of service, that is their choice, their journey. I have my role and they have theirs.

Very few of my family members are *in service* to liberation (I say this in the hopes that by the time this is published some will have moved towards being *in service* to collective liberation). Very few others around me are truly there, though many are training and visioning to be able to some day. Regardless of others' journeys, my commitment and service is to liberation, has been for a long time. I will have family, friends, coworkers, and many others who are not fully living up to being *in service* to liberation. However, they are secondary to my work.

In my early 30s my mom said an iconic statement, like she often does the few days a year we share space. She said "you have always done everything for everyone else". She was not saying this as a positive or a compliment. I have been called naive and all kinds of other names to symbolize that my kindness is not smart or strategic, which says a lot about the world we live in.

Someone asked me recently what my definition of freedom is and I shared that when I think of collective freedom or collective liberation I envision a world free from any barriers for people to be all that they are meant to be and can ever be.

To be *in service* to liberation is not only to be *in service* to a far away destination where those barriers are removed, rather it is in working to remove the barriers today.

****

All around us barriers can be removed, sometimes with ease, so that we may claim our own liberation on our way to a collectively liberated world. But most people are not *in service* to liberation, so when called upon it is seen as "too much work", "someone else's problem", "not the priority", and so many other excuses.

Service is a lifelong commitment. Being *in service* means that even when it's inconvenient, and hard, and has consequences, I do it anyway because if I remove this barrier today someone else doesn't have to go through it.

My work took an enormous turn in 2020, because prior to COVID-19 the vast majority of funders told me what I was trying to do in the world was "cute" and they funded "important work". My work did not change in 2020, the perception of things like mutual aid, utopia building, and collective liberation work did, and all of a sudden my work was fundable. Now, I work with funders who trust me to lead work that they do not understand but have learned is, in fact, what is needed.

Systems of oppression tell us that there are "right" and "wrong" ways of doing liberatory work, and most do not realize that the systems we are trying to dismantle should never be the ones telling us how to do this work.

To be *in service* to liberation requires that I understand and witness barriers. To be *in service* is to break any faith I have in systemic oppression. To be *in service* to liberation is to do the deconditioning work so that I am not a barrier. To be *in service* to liberation is to find more strategic ways to target more barriers. To be *in service* to liberation is to design my life for my mission. If life is made of work, loved ones, hobbies, and purpose then they all must align with my service to liberation.

It's hard, I know. I have cut off family members due to this misalignment. I have changed careers, hobbies, everything. I do not hold onto those losses and resent liberation, I only resent systemic oppression.

My commitment to liberation persists, regardless of any other circumstances. I am *in service* to liberation first and foremost.

LIBERATION ISN'T ABOUT YOU

In Service to a Revolution

Perhaps it might make sense to specify which revolution, for a revolution (any revolution) on its own does not actually refer to something positive. A revolution is neutral. There are fascist revolutions and liberatory revolutions and those outside of that binary. Some could argue that what's known as the united states and many other global north states are going through the beginnings of fascist revolutions—even if they have always been fascist. A revolution is a type of transformation; it is a large-scale shift in society as a whole and it is not easily reversed. The current fascist infrastructure being built is not going to be easily reversed, especially because it is built on an imperialist foundation that allows fascism to thrive.

The Revolution I am referring to is The Revolution that moves us towards collective liberation, a transformation away from imperialist nation states and into Indigenous sovereignty that centers relationship with land, spirit, and caring for one another.

A revolution is not a partial reckoning with the state of affairs and accepting whatever is considered "good enough". A revolution is an entire shift, it is large scale. A revolution changes life as we know it. There is no "we have a revolution over a weekend and back at the office the next day at 8AM". There is no "my kids will be on time to school the next day". There is no "I am going to invade Mexico City on vacation" the following week. There is no "I'm proposing to my partner with a stone that cost countless people their lives and we're spending six figures on a wedding for people we mostly dislike later in the year". There is no business as usual because business no longer exists in the way it did prior. If all these things still exist in the exact same way then we had a protest, not a revolution.

This is not to say protests are not crucial pieces of disruption and amplification, it is saying that a protest is not a revolution, even though when many people think of revolution they think of a large protest or a riot. History often immortalizes a single moment of glory, erasing the before and after, ensuring we do not have the blueprints to replicate the large-scale event.

A riot is a large-scale disturbance of the status quo, often with fire and property damage because capitalism cares more about businesses than people. Riots can be part of revolutions but they also can technically uphold the status quo—look at sports riots for example. Property damage without an anti-capitalist framework is just property damage. Setting a fire without an anti-systemic oppression framework is just pyromania. This isn't to say that good organizers can't take actions that are founded in oppressive frameworks and utilize them strategically to move us towards a liberatory revolution.

But a revolution is neither a riot nor a protest alone. A revolution is a cultural transformation that yields immense societal transformation. When a riot tears apart every starbucks and the response is no longer "how dare you harm property?" then we have begun moving towards cultural transformation.

The Revolution does not accidentally happen one day, it requires service. The Revolution requires cultural transformation, infrastructure building, escalation, and various other things that allow it to happen and be successful.

Cultural Transformation

The cultural revolution begins decades before the rioting that might be a part of the revolution. Culture is constantly shifting around us, but a cultural transformation is a large-scale shift from the status quo and is not easily reversed. Culture workers are individuals who recognize that and work through arts, education, healing practice, and various other modalities to move us towards that large-scale shift from the status quo. Again, like with everything else, transformation is neutral and sometimes culture workers will move us towards fascism instead of liberation.

So what is the culture we are working to transform? Every system, whether oppressive or otherwise, has a culture, a set of social behaviors, traditions, ways of thinking. White supremacy has a culture. Patriarchy has a culture. Capitalism has a culture. Ableism has a culture. Transphobia has a culture. And so on and so forth. As stated previously, culture is constantly in flux. Culture is not necessarily fact. Culture is the stories that are told and the influence they have in our lives.

When social behavior is modified slightly and is then branded as transformation it allows the many to embrace the immediate gratification that follows and move away from true transformation. After a small victory (for example, the marriage equality win in the supreme court), many might assume that a system of oppression no longer exists. We have seen this in every generation and at every stage.

When culture is transformed, there is no going back easily.

Without the culture work we never move past small scale disruptions that might move certain things forward but will never lead to The Revolution. Part of the difference between cultural transformation and culture change is the level of depth that we bring to understanding the systems of oppression that we are aiming to severely disrupt and how far we are moving towards a liberatory culture in the process.

For example, there is often a debate about funding and The Revolution. In my day to day work with organizing communities in what's known as the united states or other global north countries, the book *The Revolution Will Not Be Funded* comes up. The book is brought forward predominantly by individuals who have not read the book and who assume that the book is saying to not accept funding for any organizing. This comes up weekly in my world leading to an organizing culture built on volunteerism and scarcity. Many culturally believe that to maintain equity and justice within communities we can not have funding because it is funding that moves us towards inequitable systems. These thoughts are all culture. This culture influences the way that we interact with one another; the way we view resources and resource redistribution; and the way we understand capitalism, the non-profit industrial complex, and equity.

I write about this often because it continues coming up and we have not shifted this culture. Money within capitalism is always going to be blood money. Capitalism requires the use of blood money and other stolen resources to survive. The assumption that it is somehow equitable to not use said blood money to support individuals' survival within communities is devoid of actual analysis and can be really harmful. This is not saying to accept money from the most evil of places. This is saying that even my salary as the executive director of a non-profit, where all the funding comes from radical funders is still blood money. All money within capitalism is blood money, that does not change if I am not getting paid to do this work. Not accepting funds while putting my life at risk will not end capitalism. To me, this is similar to a white upper middle class individual deciding to live off grid without a job in order to protest capitalism. That is not a protest against capitalism, that is just privilege and wanting to be like generations of your ancestors who did not work and lived off grid while their money grew due to Black and Brown labor.

I don't share this to say "accept blood money". I am saying an analysis that stops with whether or not you are accepting funds is not the cultural transformation that will lead to The Revolution. How we move through resources matters—that can lead to cultural transformation. I believe in resource redistribution so that the most marginalized of the most marginalized are able to do the organizing work sustainably—that will lead us to The Revolution. I don't believe in accepting funds that have any strings attached. I believe in relationship building and culture change work over a longer period of time to make no strings attached funding possible and getting the right resources into our communities. I believe in people buying each other houses, paying rent for one another, investing in community healers, growing our own food, expanding access to social, medical, and reproductive care, and so much more. I believe in community care, but community care is not depleting one another of our resources, it is about doing more with less because these systems ensure we always have less.

All of this is about transforming culture around funds. I know we are not there yet because over the last few years, as I have spoken in over a hundred communities—in front of tens of thousands of people—when I ask if folks feel cared for by their community only three hands have ever been raised, two of whom were sisters who have always taken care of one another.

I feel cared for. I do not pay my own rent, but I pay other people's. I have access to food as I provide access to food for others. It's the same for medical care and for healing work. Some might ask what is the difference between not paying your own rent to then pay that rent for someone else. The difference is community. The difference is cultural transformation. When we take care of only ourselves we are alone.

When we take care of each other we move towards collectivism which is a cultural transformation. Capitalism and other systems of oppression can not survive collectivism.

To be *in service* to The Revolution that will move us towards a liberated world **we must recognize the importance of culture work that leads to cultural transformation.** Being *in service* to The Revolution requires that we transform the parts of us that need to be transformed so we may be ready for the day after The Revolution.

Infrastructure Building

Did you know that you can rebuild the foundation of a building as it continues standing? Little by little it can be remade. You can even move an entire building without it falling over. What would it look like if we were to rebuild the foundation of the global north entirely? As if we're termites that not only take apart but also rebuild.

This is not advocating for exclusively working within the system or saying that these systems can be saved—not at all. This is saying that we can strategically build infrastructure that is founded on liberation principles to replace systems of oppression in a liberated world.

I often ask during my talks and training "what happens if systems of oppression are dismantled today, would we know how to live and be?"

Do we know how to feed 8 billion people? Do we know how to even be around one another interpersonally? We do not need all the answers, but we need infrastructure that will replace the current systems. As we build this infrastructure we are able to move towards and be *in service* to The Revolution.

So, what does it mean to build infrastructure? It means building systems that serve us and are able to meet our needs. There are countless examples of communities building infrastructure, from resource redistribution pathways to transformative justice. We have always had to build external infrastructure to survive. It should come as no surprise that infrastructure is one of the areas most heavily targeted by systems of oppression, as it serves as one of the biggest threats against them.

When I say infrastructure, I mean that we have something already set for us to utilize when needed. At the height of my infrastructure for queer and trans folks most impacted by genocide, I had the funds to evacuate anyone as long as borders were open, provide support for basic and non-basic needs, pay months of rent for individuals targeted, and in limited cases even hire individuals with a full salary so they may center their organizing work instead of attempting to survive capitalism. I could offer pathways for QT organizers impacted by genocide that the system does not even offer to cis-straight white individuals.

I say at the height of my infrastructure because it was severely damaged by unhealed community members. This will happen again to other infrastructure, because until we radically transform our culture of care and are *in service* to The Revolution, our infrastructure is frail at best, torn apart by state and/or community violence.

I build infrastructure in a way that allows for these attacks to not dismantle the entire thing, but infrastructure is needed in enormous scales and can not be led by a single vision. I don't know many people invested in building this infrastructure; often it is me building it with support from others but I am the only one responsible for it. If I am assassinated most of it disappears (some doesn't because of how it's built, but a lot does).

What infrastructure do you have in your communities? When you need access to your basic needs do you have a system in place to support you and others or is it a makeshift individualized response? Individual responses will never be enough. We're talking about a revolution, we're talking about tens of millions impacted. Who cares for the children whose parents are killed in the process? Who will feed the tens of millions who lose all access to food? What is schooling during the revolution? How do the tens of millions of disabled people get medical care? Where do you get your medication?

Individuals will often ask me where to start with infrastructure building. My answer is always start at home. What do you need? What can you give? What systems don't serve you? What systems do you have the skill set to build? Don't think about somewhere else—not yet. If you're students let's talk student loans, let's talk housing, let's talk food insecurity. How do you create an alternative where folks are cared for? If you

155

build it for students you can expand it to the encampment outside the ivory gates. If you expand it to unhoused neighbors you can expand it to those barely holding onto housing. Little by little, one block at a time we replace the existing infrastructure.

But most of our current movements are not *in service* to The Revolution. Out of the hundreds of encampments that launched in the spring of 2024 only one that I know of fully integrated with their neighbors.

Infrastructure building is not a priority for most of our spaces. We do not have the skill sets to build deeply rooted infrastructure. And when it is built, the attacks externally and internally destroy it faster than we can rebuild. Regardless, we must prioritize long term infrastructure building in a way that does not get dismantled by every attack—unfortunately sometimes from our own people. The person who harmed my infrastructure the most in 2024 was a trans Palestinian I trusted. The person who harmed it the most in 2025 was a Global Majority Trans Muslim. I don't believe either was malicious. I believe our people are hurt and broken in ways where they do not know how to filter light in and instead cut one another while doing their "best". This is why we must be better broken as we move to being *in service*. This is why we must be *in service* and build resilient infrastructure.

Escalation

Y'all didn't think we were going to talk about revolution and not talk about setting things on fire and property damage—about violence.

To be clear, any type of resistance will be seen as violent by systems of oppression and those who serve them. And, violence from systems of oppression will only ever increase. They begin with violence, endure through violence, and they go out with violence. Some say that this is the end of Empire, and Empire thrashes with violence as it dies. That may be true, but the Empire is violent—has always been. To assume all violence is equal is a way to avoid responsibility for building a liberated world.

So many people are abundantly anti-violence within the movement.

Violence is an anti-violent tool that allows us to prevent future violence. Violence in movements is like controlled burns in forests to prevent the entire forest from being burned. No one who is truly here for liberation wants to burn down parts of a forest, but we do out of love for the collective.

So, how do we prepare for violence?

Violence is never a starting point, at least not if you want to be strategic. Violence is a specific tool for liberation.

Every once in a while someone will ask me about violence at an event or after an event. Some want me to denounce my people's resistance—those don't get a response—but sometimes it's individuals who genuinely want to better understand where violence fits into organizing.

My response is usually along the lines of "what work have you done?" The amount of work we have to do to build a healthy foundation and build our capacity before we may engage in violence is immense, and I do not waste my time. I am here for strategy. There is very little I am opposed to, but I am here for strategy. I am here for folks being trained, I am here for experience.

Training and experience is critical to have because these are the things that allow us to find the right co-conspirators—it's not safe to engage in conversation about violence against the system with the wrong people. Even writing this section puts me at risk in a multitude of ways (for all intents and legal purposes I am not advocating for individual violence).

We need to do the work to be able to work with violence. Violence might not be necessary, but if we need to destroy property, set things on fire, or other escalations, then we need to be prepared.

Escalations don't have to be violent, but we have to be ready for the extremes of what it takes to remake the world. We must escalate.

There are many places I work with who have zero organizing infrastructure: Their definition of organizing is fundraising and event planning—both critical areas but are not organizing. Those communities have not organized any disruptions. Escalating for them would be moving from permit protests to disruptions. Disruptions can start with inconveniencing others and then escalating to shutting down bridges, airports, etc. Shutting down bridges and airports then leads to mass organized strikes. This isn't a step by step, these things can happen synchronously. There are thousands of types of actions, the key is to always utilize a combination of tactics that are constantly increasing in building pressure. Ultimately, it's not a fire that will save us. We can shut down every airport, that means nothing if everyone returns to airports tomorrow. The assignment is disrupting in a way that will lead to cultural transformation and building infrastructure.

****

There are various other areas that are central to being *in service* to The Revolution. I focused on the foundational elements, but there are so many others.

Being *in service* to The Revolution means **finding my role** in The Revolution—something we all have—and then **investing** into that revolutionary future. If I invest in systemic oppression I will not be ready for The Revolution that is meant to dismantle it. If my entire world is to invest in a workplace that upholds capitalism and my relationships aren't liberatory then I haven't done the work to be ready for The Revolution, I am not *in service* to The Revolution.

The Revolution is risky, it bears potential consequences. The act of the revolution and the aftermath bear consequences— there is also a large payout in the form of a collectively liberated world.

I believe in The Revolution and more importantly, the world we build after it. I am *in service* to this future. I can only live where I am *in service* to it. Every relationship must be an investment in that world. Every word I write and say is *in service*. I am *in service*.

THERE IS NO COLLECTIVE LIBERATION WITHOUT SERVICE

In Service To Land

My favorite memory of all time (and yes I know that I am young and whatever) is of running as a four or five year old in a wheatgrass field that would later become my grandparents' house. I have written so much about this field, even in a future utopia in *Inara: light of utopia*. This memory is not real, for every time we remember we are also embellishing, and I have remembered this memory so much over the decades that I have a little less of the actual memory every time. I remember joy. I remember pee. I remember devastation.

This memory is so integral because it is the first memory I have of nature, of land.

I was born in a major city, Amman, Jordan. At the time Amman was quickly being developed to accommodate the over a million Palestinians who had been displaced from Kuwait post The Gulf War. My parents and many of their immediate family were part of that. Those with wealth moved into the original mountains of Amman, closer to The Balad or to newer posh areas that were expansions beyond these mountains. Those without wealth were moved towards the refugee camps. Sweileh became a Palestinian hub very quickly at that time, and to this day it is seen as a middle ground between the camps and the rest of Amman. I want to honor that Amman has an extensive history, each neighborhood telling a different part of the story, but for the sake of this essay I am simplifying it to be able to share the position I was born in. I was born in Sweileh.

At the time of my birth, Sweileh was a mix of apartment buildings and independent stone houses. Over the years, Sweileh has become a concrete jungle of buildings jutting out and connecting to one another: on one side overlooking a valley that ends with a Palestinian refugee camp, on another side is one of the richest neighborhoods where the Royal Family currently resides; another side moves you towards the university, and the final side moves you to Salt. Sweileh is at the very edge of Amman, bordering Salt and Ein Al-Basha.

Ein Al-Basha is where this story starts. It is the part of the valley in between Sweileh and The Refugee camp, at the time there was beautiful farmland and fields as far as the eye can see. Today, there are a few farms and as far as the eye can see there are buildings, smaller than what you'd find in Sweileh or closer to the seven hills of Amman, but it doesn't resemble the land I peed my pants on as a child.

I am currently writing this in the field of my childhood, but the field is only a memory. Instead, there is an acre of land fenced with grey stone bricks, half the land is the house my grandfather died in and where my grandmother is currently napping. The other half is my grandfather's garden, and although it is no longer a field of wheatgrass, it is its own slice of paradise with olive, fig, almond, eskadenia, berry, lemon, pomegranate, cactus, and other trees that I surely have missed. This is the first time that I write in this home of mine.

My grandfather did not allow anyone except my grandmother and my sisters and I to be in this garden. After his passing in 2020, the trees claimed the space and it was only recently that my aunt dedicated time to caring for it again.

I am in sacred space, his and mine in very different ways. I came here today to take branches from his trees to grow on land I am conserving not too far from here.

When it comes to being *in service* I recognize that land is one of the most important areas, and I recognize that it is one of the areas where I have done the least. This was the field that brought me to nature, my first experience of meeting land.

Then, at the age of 6, we moved to Tempe, Arizona, a suburb. There were trees along the sidewalks, but they were filled with the threat of the cops being called on you if you looked at them or wanted to pick an orange or pomegranate (I was 6 and 7 and 8 and 9-12).

We moved to Ontario, Canada, and again lived in an urban city. Then back to Amman, a different area than Sweileh but just as many buildings. The north of Jordan, the south of Syria: all buildings, and though the land between the two countries is green, I rarely noticed in my delirious dissociative unhoused years.

Then, in central Massachusetts for college there was a lot more nature, but four jobs on campus meant I was just on campus. Things changed towards the end of my sophomore year. I was doing a co-op at an engineering firm and one of my co-workers—in his mid-40s, married with two kids—started inviting me out to hikes. I saw more forests and mountains with him than I ever had before. We remained friends through my junior year. I didn't realize that he was trying to sleep with me the entire time, but I saw trees and so much sky. I'm grateful for that time. He blocked me when he realized I was not going to sleep with him, but it was too late by then, I had finally witnessed and been in nature, and I never stopped.

It's one thing to witness nature, it's another to be *in service* to land. For years, I have thought about how I contribute to the environment, not just from a "how am I killing land?" but also "how am I actively investing in land?"

I travel for work, I've been on thousands of planes; the footprint of that alone is immense. I use technology for work, that alone has cost lives in The Congo and other places that bear the brunt of owning this laptop I'm writing on. I eat out, so there's all that plastic. I do not own a car because years ago I decided I was not going to wait for perfect public transportation to do the little I can. Not having a car in what's known as Waterbury, CT, is definitely not as ideal as Belfast or Oakland, but it was what I could and wanted to do.

I have yearned for years to claim my agrarian roots and grow my own food, not ideal without a yard or access to land. I tried growing my own herbs once from an herb kit. I left for a month to care for my sister with stage 4 cancer and they were dead when I got back.

Last year, I decided to take every penny I had anywhere to buy a small plot of olive trees to conserve. My best friends helped me cover the rest of the cost. Now there are olive trees overlooking Falasteen, safe from development. I will take from Seedo's trees to plant with the olive trees and they will all overlook Falasteen.

What does it mean to be *in service* to land when I am incredibly harmful to land? Specifically, what does it mean to be *in service* to land when I am almost entirely in cities, where organizing is needed most, away from any nature? I struggle with this, yearnings pulling me in different directions. On one hand I feel one with land and I want to be in nature but I recognize that the places where organizing is needed most are in the midst of concrete. I can sit in Seedo's slice of paradise, lay here and even sleep between the trees but the threat to this and most land is not here. The threat is in papers being signed in what's known as washington, d.c. and new york city, the hague, london, berlin, beijing, and so many other cities.

My service to land has been organizing to dismantle the systems targeting land. I have done environmental justice work for years but it doesn't feel like I am truly *in service* unless I am connected beyond the concrete. But maybe that's just ego desiring comfort, and liberation is pulling me towards knowing that to be *in service* is to sometimes be away from the thing you are *in service* to.

I would love to live on a plot of land where I can reclaim my family's agrarian background, where I can feed others, but I am currently called to serve far away from

167

home often, training in the places very few organizers with my skill sets travel to. But this isn't about me. Soon, my disability and work will intersect and I will host retreats and intensive trainings at home instead of on the road. Until then, I understand my role.

I sit with the question of service to land, now thousands of miles away from Seedo's garden, on stolen land, knowing that my service is different here than it would be on my people's land.

Stewarding land, fighting against those oppressing the land, and becoming an extension of the land is determined by positionality, indigeneity, and the service we are in.

The land is an extension of its inhabitants and caretakers. We can not claim to be *in service* to land when we are not *in service* to indigenous sovereignty and all living beings.

Stewarding Land

Stewarding land is everyone's responsibility. However, it always happens with the guidance of the original caretakers of that place. To conserve on this stolen land is a very different process than stewarding land near my home. Conserving stolen land without the original caretakers is land theft by a different name.

Stewarding land is an extension of caring for the people of the land, and vice versa—one can not happen without the other. Conserving land is a part of stewarding land but it is not the entirety. Conserving land is the start—we begin by protecting land—stewarding is the continued care of the land today, tomorrow, and everyday for as long as we have a relationship with it. We are always in relationship with land. Neither protecting nor stewarding happens on stolen land without the guidance of the communities indigenous to the land.

Without the guidance and involvement of those communities, conserving and stewarding land are colonial tools. Colonial tools that have been used for hundreds of years, on Abya Yala, Falasteen, Haiti, and so many parts of the world. But land stewardship can also be used to decolonize and heal the wounds of colonialism and settler-colonialism. We move with intention and we care for all along the way. Part of that care might be to unsettle. Service varies by person, and just like this is not the right time for me to grow food on the land, you might not be the right person to steward stolen land if your ancestors are the ones who aimed to end Indigenous stewardship in the first place. Perhaps, through relationships with indigenous communities you are tasked for a specific form of service. We (settlers) do not define our service to stolen land, the land and its people do.

Stewarding land is also not about growing food on local land. If you gentrify then you are in contradiction to stewarding land. If you own land/housing and there is no plan for it to be transferred to Indigenous communities then you are in contradiction to stewarding land. If you are actively taking destructive transportation options then you are in contradiction to stewarding land. Of course, if you are on stolen land and you promote fascism and a vision of extracting from the land, you are in contradiction to stewarding land.

Often, we think of stewarding land in rural communities where there are thousands of empty acres of land, but stewarding land happens every day on all land, even in the middle of the biggest cities. Our responsibility does not end because we have extensively inhabited land. In fact, it's more important to care for land that has been harmed so that we may tend it into the future.

Fighting against those oppressing the land

I embody an Islamic practice of war: the only two justified reasons for violence are self-defense and to stand against oppression. Attempting to steward land or even just conserve it while upholding a fascist state is not being *in service* to land. The greatest threat to land everywhere is the imperialist white supremacist patriarchal empires. Attempting to conserve land without this awareness ends with the planet being destroyed. Conserving land is a short term strategy to alleviate the negative impacts of the colonial project. I'm not just talking about the empire that calls itself the united states, I am talking about the entirety of the global north, I am talking about china, I am talking about all the empires killing our world. I can not be in service to land and stand with those who are actively destroying land.

There are far too many projects that come my way for land conservation or creating farms for the community. Most of the individuals involved in these projects are searching for individual liberation, not collective liberation. We are tired of living under capitalism, white supremacy, and so many other systems of oppression. Most of these projects are a way for individuals to move away from cities that are oppressive to them to other stolen land where the oppression affects them less.

I get it, I also want to leave these systems behind. But moving away under the guise of service to land is individualistic, and a privilege that the most marginalized of the most marginalized do not have. If conserving land or starting a farm, even if led by marginalized individuals, does not mean that now we have additional capacity for the fight so that all marginalized people have access to what we do then we are not *in service* to land. We should and we must conserve land, start farming projects, and even intentional communities, but the purpose must always be to dismantle systems of oppression. Otherwise, we've mostly just *in service* to ourselves.

Being *in service* to land is political. There is no aspect of service to revolution, land, or any of the other areas that dedicate our lives to collective liberation that is not political, and that is not connected to the others.

Becoming an extension of the land

In Islam we believe bodies are borrowed and as soon as we die they are to be returned to the land where they can nourish future generations. I love this practice, except for the fact that now our bodies are actually poisonous to the land without some kind of intervention like a mycelium suit. What we put into our bodies matters. How we live our lives matters. Being *in service* to land is not separate from caring for the rest of our being. We are an extension of land. Our bodily autonomy is an extension of the autonomy in the land.

Far too many organizers die in their service to liberation, never realizing that a non-strategic death is not *in service* to liberation, The Revolution, or to land. Our service requires a commitment to both our beings and the community. Ideally, the two commitments align, creating a culture of service that permeates all around us.

There are many ways that this plays out. When we honor our bodyminds as an extension of the land then we are able to have solid foundations for the work and to expand our capacity to organize—both within communities that are committed to service to land and communities that are not.

When our bodyminds are an extension of land then we move through organizing in ways that are not *unintentionally* detrimental to us. I say unintentionally because we can strategically put our bodyminds in harm's way in our service. For example, I know traveling in the ways that I do harms my body AND in my travels

I raise hundreds of thousands of dollars and interact with tens of thousands of people that otherwise would not have access to the things I share about liberation work. Longterm, it is not strategic for me to destroy my body entirely beyond functionality and where I am no longer *in service* to anything.

A large part of my work is in building liberatory spaces where the culture is a commitment to being an extension of land. Most individuals coming into these spaces come to them without their own individual commitments. At the beginning of working together individuals have called into meetings with the flu, covid, from the ER, immediately after a heart attack or stroke, in between chemo, and so on. The calls were not critical calls, and it was not a conscious decision to show up, rather everyone felt like they had to due to prior conditioning.

I myself have done many of these things. The last time was in June 2020, as I was in excruciating pain due to salmonella and I used my cane to prop myself up to facilitate a training. The training was not critical, and even though this was a time where the money from the training helped I did not have to do this. I did not know I had a choice. For the last five years I have made sure that others know that they have a choice. I have also done extensive work to support others to move towards liberatory management of nervous systems so that they can know the difference between when something is an emergency and when something is not.

Part of being *in service* to land is working with our bodyminds to be more strategic in our service. For example, our stress response during times of crises allows us to expand our capacity for a short period of time. If we treat everything as an emergency then that natural stress response no longer increases our capacity—in fact, over time it causes severe damage to our bodies. Our bodies are a part of land and they, like the land, are not disposable. Every breath is a reminder of that. I am an extension of land, as my bodymind moves towards liberation and balance then I am moving towards being *in service* to land. When I am *in service* to land then my bodymind is also moving towards liberation and balance.

****

To be *in service* to land is to be intentional about how we move in the world and the world we are investing in. None of this work can happen without being *in service* to land. We can not be *in service* to liberation and revolution without being *in service* to land. We fight against those oppressing land by being *in service* to revolution. If we harm land irreparably there won't be a world to liberate. Our movements must be *in service* to land, our revolution must be *in service* to land. We must be *in service* to land.

NOTHING IS TO BE WASTED

In Service to Community

I struggle with community. I struggle with something I have never physically had and yet have always been spiritually bonded with. I was born *in* and *of* community, it just seems that for most of my life no one else *in* and *of* community recognized that I was. In most ways, I have been treated as an outsider my entire life.

Even before my first displacement I never fit in. I didn't talk enough or at all at times. I bit my tongue when I was mad. I ran away constantly. But it was more than that. No matter who I came in contact with, they thought I was out of place, thinking I was foreign in one way or another.

Post first displacement that foreignness led to white women calling the cops on me as a child, but even in my smaller predominantly Black and Brown immigrant community I was different. I don't think I look that different but even at home in Falasteen an artist from Nazareth asked the friend I was with "if our people look like this?" She was a beautiful and kind soul and I can not imagine a world where her soul carries malice but the message was clear. I am different. Only a single person has ever told me I look like my people.

But it's so much more than looks.

I learned to use my otherness, finding power in my margins and playing the role that only an outsider can play within the current ways our communities operate. As an outsider I can say things that others within the community might be fearful to say due to negative repercussions; even when there are no repercussions, the community might not be ready for the new relationship gifted with conflict. Some communities also learn to value "the foreign" more than their own when it comes to specific types of expertise, often listening to outside voices far more than their own. When I enter a new community I enter as an expert. When I exist in my own physical community I am a number, another one of many. There is a reason that most of my work is usually not where I live, no matter how much I yearn for that to change.

I used to yearn to be a part of mainstream community, but along the way I have realized that being on the margins means I witness the broader community from the outside, allowing me to see the areas of growth needed and the others on the margins of community—some more marginalized than me. Being *in service* to community has meant building space for others like me on the margins so that we may always have space to share as a community. Most of my work—if not all of it, has been on the margins of marginalization.

Yet, I am still in service to the broader community. The work on the margins is the most transformative because it causes a ripple effect from the outside in, reaching everyone. When work exists in the center of the mainstream the ripple might only reach the inner most layers of privilege, not those on the outside.

Community can mean many things. I am often asked how I define it and I mention the various layers of community. To me, there's the interpersonal layer, the broader ecosystem, the broader macro, and the transcendental levels.

The interpersonal are the people in our actual orbit, we know them and they know us. We love them and they love us because we have actual relationships with them. They can be family, friends, pets, house plants, trees you have immediate access to. This is the orbit where you are in relationship.

The broader ecosystem are the people orbiting our orbit or a community we connect with. We do not know everyone at this level and most likely will never meet everyone, but we are connected through our interpersonal relationships.

The broader macro level is the community of people we will never know. It is hundreds of millions of people to billions of people, constellations of people impacted by our existence in ways we will never know.

The transcendental level is when we move away from community being defined by human relationships. Community is about land, spirit, and everything else in existence. Community can even be of thoughts and actions, stars and the cosmos, and energy we may never understand.

Community is all of these levels. It is not one level alone, a single level is like having hydrogen compounds without the oxygen in water. It is incomplete.

To be *in service* to community we must be *in service* to all of these levels. To do that we must move towards collectivism, beyond likability politics, and towards care and being responsible for one another.

Collectivism

I speak a lot about the interpersonal level in regards to collectivism and how if we stop at the interpersonal level we're actually individualistic and not collectivist. If our entire understanding of community is defined by direct relationships then our understanding of community is ego and attachment driven. It is when we start showing up for the things we do not have direct relationships with that we are truly moving towards collectivism. Collectivism is being *in service* to community, rather than being *in service* to our ego.

A good friend of mine recently shared that she's in relationship with her ego and nourishes her ego, but the ego is not the center of her universe. I appreciate this outlook compared to the ego death narratives that we often hear and I myself am guilty of upholding. I still believe in ego death, however, death is a relationship. Recognizing that the ego is a part of us, that it has a role to play, is a beautiful way of community building. However, we are not *in service* of our egos, we are *in service* of community and the ego may be a part of that.

My ego is the part of me that tells me I exist, that I matter, I am lovable and I deserve to take up space and attention. When I talk about ego death I am referring to a relationship with my ego where these things are irrelevant in liberation work, but that does not mean that the entire relationship with my ego is dependent on ego death. Our egos can be beautiful and transformative parts of our work. For example, if in my service I am building spaces that cultivate belonging but I feel as if I do not exist and matter then I have not built a place that cultivates belonging. If liberatory relationships are loving and I don't feel loved and held by community then have we built liberatory relationships? Liberatory relationships do not demand the death of the ego; in fact, liberatory relationships allow the ego to be held and balanced. Feeling a sense of belonging and that I matter is beautiful and can serve as a blueprint for the culture we need to build for a collectively liberated world. At the same time, when we are in spaces where me existing is not the priority then the ego might move us in unstrategic ways. We all want to matter, but if my desire to matter is greater than the liberation work then I am not in healthy relationship with my ego or the work. In that case I begin to serve my ego, not liberation. The truth is: I matter, but no where near as much as liberation work. Within liberatory relationships we balance the two, reducing the possibility that our egos will harm the work while moving towards building a world where we all matter.

When we are *in service* to our ego we are *in service* to individualism, not collectivism, because in that case I matter more than the collective. Collectivism is being *in service* to community. Collectivism is not just being connected to a broader ecosystem, it is dedicating our lives and being to that community.

It's unfortunate that so many of us are so far removed from community—it is by design and is intentional. Systems of oppression can not survive community.

Beyond Likability Politics

What would it be like to live in a community where no one is disposable? A community where your likability did not determine your worth? I lived in a community like that for a few years as a child, none of us with enough privilege to discard one another, where we all needed one another to survive. The adults around me at the time did not always like each other, and when they liked each other it wasn't very relevant. Survival demanded labor, everyone found what they could do, defined by the community's needs and their skill sets.

When Seedo, my dad's dad, used to tell us stories of Falasteen pre-1948 he spoke of similar communities. He would tell us that at the time people drank from the same cup in the mosque—something I found disgusting at the time (face palm). We talked about disability justice and queer justice without ever calling them that. Everyone had a role to play in his world. I yearn to be in a community in that way. I know the community wasn't perfect in his world—but I'm not yearning for perfection, I'm yearning for a community that's able to move past likability politics and build with one another, where we all have different roles and a shared service for liberation.

Likability politics impact every part of community building, especially conflict, accountability, and growth.

182

If someone we like causes harm our response is often different than if we do not like them. If the person harmed is someone we like, the response is different than if the person harmed is someone we do not.

We want to like one another to have relationships but those relationships are meant to move us towards liberation, not away from one another. Likability is a pathway to move towards accountability, but is often used to do the opposite. Systems of oppression—each of them—teach us to like certain groups of people (not always the most privileged). Systems of oppression also teach us that since identities are meant to be liked at different times likability serves as a shield from accountability and growth. For example, post October 7th 2023 I received immense likability privilege as a Palestinian, so much so that others found it difficult to challenge me. I've seen this happen with plenty of Palestinians, at times resulting in disaster for the community. There is no one group that is perfect and does not need to move towards accountability and to grow. Accountability and growth are essential for being *in service* to community. Liberation must be built on a sacred understanding of human nature: we make mistakes, we move towards accountability, and grow—or we choose not to and move away from liberation.

Care and Responsibility for One Another

When no one is disposable then everyone is cared for—it's actually that simple. When we feel responsible for one another and thus are *in service* to one another then everyone is cared for.

Within white supremacist capitalist systems it's difficult to talk about care beyond the realities of surviving capitalism. I see dozens of crowd sourcing campaigns every time I open social media (despite rarely scrolling). Hundreds fill my DMs, and it feels as if every single day other organizers and loved ones have their own campaigns. Capitalism is literally killing us — quickly in some places through genocide and very slowly in others through our labor. Most care that we discuss these days is in financial support for all our basic necessities due to capitalism.

Care isn't exclusive to financial support; in fact, outside of capitalism monetary exchanges are not the dominant interaction. Care is about how we emotionally support one another, how we support one another's growth, how we hold each other accountable, how we invest in a future for all of us.

But do we feel responsible for one another? It's easy to step away when someone harms. It's easy to step away when someone isn't likeable. It's easy to step away when capitalism tells us that it can replace community. White supremacy tells us it will save us. Patriarchy tells us that if we need anyone it's just family, led by a man in a nuclear family; he'll provide and protect you and if he doesn't, you fail. They all lie, even when it seems as if they're honest in the short term due to the benefits they provide, but it's only immediate gratification, and we spend a lifetime working to feel it again.

At the same time, capitalism has conditioned us to believe that all work is capitalist, as if service is not a part of daily reality in a liberated world. I am often berated for using the word work because most people hear an ableist capitalist concept. But the problem isn't with work. Work is beautiful, it is necessary. Work looks different from person to person, not just in our abilities and skill sets but because our communities need different things. Our roles evolve with our communities, we are not meant to be stagnant and unmoved by the way that our worlds are evolving.

****

I'm sad writing this chapter. Our communities are in a lot of pain, I get that. In the words of my editor, Mays Salamah "we're yearning for stronger community whether we know it or not—it really is sad". Every one of these forms of service is an entry point into the others. Service to community seems like a beautiful start point. I hope it's a start point on our paths to collective liberation.

186

CAPITALISM CANNOT SURVIVE COLLECTIVISM

In Service to the Most Marginalized of the Most Marginalized

Initially, this entire book was going to be about being *in service* to the most marginalized of the most marginalized. If you ask me what the foundation of my work is I would probably tell you a lot of different forms of marginalization that I use as methodologies for my organizing. I use Islamic spirituality, transness, disability, queerness, displacement, racialization, and Indigeneity as methodologies for how to move through the world. I even use death as a methodology.

At the core of all of these is a space of overlap where my compass is constantly pointed towards the most marginalized of the most marginalized.

I didn't learn this as a theory, I learned this through my life. My people, Palestinians specifically, have been marginalized my entire life and for generations prior. I was born as the third generation of displaced family members destined to not go home unless the world is liberated. I was born as a Global South citizen, but I was born a citizen of *somewhere,* which is a privilege. I was born in severe poverty. Everyone around me when I was born was living in the same forms of marginalization or additional ones depending on who they were.

I was also born autistic and trans. This meant that within the marginalizations those around me carried, I carried a few extras that then made me different. I was the child who never talked or talked too much. And I was a person who did not understand any concept of gender but was made to feel, and felt, like there was something severely wrong with me.

From the youngest of ages, I looked at the people around me from the outside. I initially tried to beg, pray, or buy my way into the community and never succeeded because I was on the margins from the very beginning. Others were even farther in the margins, where I did not see them either.

I think of marginalization as a circle with countless other rings around it, almost like a Russian doll. The center is the most privileged of the most privileged, these are the billionaires and ruling class who ultimately impact everyone else's marginalizations. As we move outwards we move farther and farther towards the most marginalized of the most marginalized.

Usually, we see those in our rings and those deeper on the inside, taught to envy them. We are conditioned to look to the inside, the allure of assimilation claiming that we can also be in the center. If we see those in the margins, it is usually to degrade and dehumanize—to feel superior. Which is to say that we don't see those at the margins at all, the most privileged see a version of the margins that only exists in their imaginations and are rooted in their justifications for why the margins are "necessary" in the first place.

My family moved to what's known as Tempe, AZ, when I was six. New layers of marginalization were compounded on my family leading to relationships with others on the margins. I grew up in the type of community built on community care, shared struggle for liberation, and a deep rooted service for survival or justice (depending on the time and community member). It's a thin line between service to survival and service to justice, even as we are shamed for our survival. I say that my community had a deeply rooted service to survival and justice because our survival was a daily struggle, and often the assumption is that by moving towards survival we are then able to move towards justice. The two are interlinked and unless you want to embrace the space between (martyrdom) one is required for the other. By that I mean that without being *in service* to survival we don't make it. However, it is not survival that leads to justice, it is justice that leads to survival. The hope of achieving justice tomorrow allows us to survive today, and justice allows us to survive as a species. Being *in service* to survival alone means that as soon as assimilation is an option our service ends. Being in service to justice exists beyond assimilation politics. My community has a mix of the two, but my immediate community were the ones who did not have the privilege to assimilate and move on. We came together to survive but survival was not the assignment, building a more just world was.

I learned so much from that community, not just in seeing what was right but also seeing what is wrong. I witnessed many of the people I grew up with move towards privilege, leaving behind everyone at the margins. I was fortunate that my family were among the few left behind, who didn't have the privilege to move towards whiteness. I recently reconnected with someone who grew up in the same community I did, similar background but with class privilege. Their experience is devoid of the magic I witnessed in my community, because for many, community care is a choice and most opt out except in egregious capitalist ways.

Then, I saw it with my own family, as my family moved towards privilege when we moved to Jordan, towards a middle class, towards assimilation, and they almost forgot about the margins. This amnesia has been present throughout my teenage and adult years and now I work with my family to help them remember; sometimes they do and other times they don't, and more often than not they remember only for the amnesia to come again in the space between our conversations. It is hard to witness the margins when everyone around you gaslights you to believe that safety only exists within assimilation.

I recognize the difficulty in moving away from the same systems that have taught you all you know and thus feel like home. But we have to do better. As I write this in Amman, where my parents live, there is a large scale transformation happening. Entire sections of Jordan are being sold to "Israel", have been for at least the 20 years I have lived here on and off. Indigenous communities here are being forced off their land to make way for the Zionist state. But people are comfortable in the capital: even my family did not know what I was able to find out in hours. It's easy to look away when you're comfortable, even as your own people are genocided.

Somedays I feel the pull of amnesia, until I look in the mirror or interact with any human and then I am reminded of who I am. It is easy to forget when pathways for assimilation are open to you. I think about class often. I have a vast experience of class, from moving from severe poverty to a lower middle class high school, to leaving home at 16/17 and experiencing levels of severe poverty that I don't have words for, becoming an adult on the streets, sex work, all kinds of work, so many jobs, being unhoused again and again and again, hospitalizations, more jobs, more jobs, more jobs, and then all of a sudden comfort? Money? Pathways to money? Although I could not assimilate into the vast majority of identities, I could assimilate within class.

I **can** assimilate within class. I can step away from everything, disappear into the world and leave all organizing behind. I have seen so many do it.

A few days ago I was lying in my grandfather's garden for hours and I thought of how easy it would be to disappear into that garden. Of course, with all the other identities I hold I can't actually disappear. I am still a disabled trans person in a garden and as soon as anyone is around, I am no longer assimilating. But then I could be in that garden with others on the margins of marginalization, and we can claim we're not assimilating, but we are. I would assimilate within individuality, neglecting every other part of the community beyond myself. I am not dissuading folks from the dream of the slice of heaven far away from the violence of the societies we currently live in. What I

193

am saying is that we are not *in service* to the most marginalized of the most marginalized or any of the other areas of service in these chapters when we claim privilege to escape.

To be *in service* to the most marginalized of the most marginalized is to always witness the most marginalized of the most marginalized, and that can't happen while moving towards the most privileged. And this does not happen through morality politics that define the margins as where "good" people are and privileged people as "bad". This binary harms us. If your family is evil and has procured generational wealth through enslavement and stealing resources then you are not a "good" person by not taking that wealth. You should take it and redistribute it equitably because you have access to it and the most marginalized do not. Moving towards the most marginalized does not mean a belief that the most marginalized are "good", it means that we each have a responsibility to end all marginalization period.

Marginalization does not make us "good" people and it does not give us purpose. Marginalization is forced upon us and in a liberated world we will be "good" people and we will have purpose. Turning your back on power unstrategically in an attempt to move towards the margins is ego and discomfort with being from a privileged class. I'm not talking about the people who can make far more money within evil organizations deciding that working at google is evil. I am talking about the individuals who refuse to redistribute the resources they have access to and instead move towards helplessness because they can't sit with the reality that they might be "bad" people as defined by these structures.

Within these binary systems of "good" and "bad", "in need", and "able to give" we move away from the reality that we all have a role to play in building a liberated world. Everyone, regardless of how marginalized, has a role to play. Within these systems, the role of the most marginalized is limited to "receiving support" or "inspiring", while in reality the most marginalized of the most marginalized have been leaders of every successful social justice movement, mutual aid network, and community care practice. But not every marginalized person is a revolutionary leader or knows how to practice mutual aid either. We all play a role, marginalization is just one piece of how we claim roles.

There are many people who want to live paycheck to paycheck but we are not the same. I live paycheck to paycheck because everything beyond my basic needs is redistributed. They live paycheck to paycheck because they refuse to accept funds for their labor. I run into this often with university speakers. The number of individuals who will speak at evil institutions but refuse to receive and redistribute funds from those institutions (to be able to continue claiming that they are struggling) is staggering. I don't want people any richer, I want resources redistributed and if you have the power to access resources and you refuse to access them and redistribute them, then to me you are just as violent as those who hoard the resources. We are not the same and those on the margins can always tell. I am not telling you to live lavishly and waste resources, I am telling you the opposite. Not many know how to move through redistributing resources.

I recognize that many of us are struggling with these questions. After all, the conditioning to be "good" is incredibly deep and a lot of us are trying to do the "good" thing. We want to be strategic and effective and we want to build a liberated world. And we struggle with the questions of power and privilege and the margins and where we are meant to show up. Often, individuals will ask me if I think X, let's say if accepting a job at a not values-aligned space is okay if they will be redistributing funds? Let's say by taking this job you are able to redistribute $25,000 a year. To me, the answer is not just a yes or no. To me, I want to invite folks to reflect on what they would need to do to be able to still have that same impact without an evil job. This might not be immediate, but if you are in an evil job for decades that is very different than doing it short term as you skill build and expand your liberatory work.

I'll give myself as an example. I have decades worth of experience in engineering, philanthropy, non-profit management, trauma work, large scale infrastructure building, managing multi-billion dollar portfolios, and consulting with entire countries. If I leave all organizing I can be making a salary between $250,000-$400,000, if not more if I really want to assimilate. I can be redistributing $150,000-$300,000 a year to communities. Those are large numbers, but they are no where near as large as the impact I have as an organizer and in the work I am currently doing. When I am in a place where my organizing is no longer worth that then it might be time to strategically move into a very different role. Any role can be made more efficient and effective. Strategy can exist in everything. Morality politics do not serve us in any way. So, what is your impact? How can you increase it? None of this is easy or immediate. Systems of oppression do not celebrate us as we move to role-clarity and efficiency. In my case, I do it because even if it becomes strategic to make that salary and redistribute, I know that my body can not survive more than two years. This extreme, for me, is what moved me towards learning how to move strategically from a young age because I didn't have the option to assimilate. Assimilation means death in my case, in more ways than I will get into here.

For a society who despises individuals living in poverty many from higher socio-economic statuses have bought into the systemically oppressive messaging that you can only be "good" if you are poor. In so many "liberatory spaces" individuals hide their wealth and access to resources to seem closer to marginalization than they really are. If you can't tell, this is a problem. Every day I see individuals on the margins trying to protect others with immense privilege without knowing that we are not the same.

Without naming our positionality and how we are moving towards privilege we are a liability for the most marginalized of the most marginalized and in our service to liberation. However, being *in service* to the most marginalized of the most marginalized does not end with witnessing this positionality. The art of witnessing is to know that people are out there struggling in ways you will never know. Witnessing is not only grasping the visible, it is grasping the invisible. Witnessing is moving away from the idea that only what is in front of me and what I know is real. I will never see the absolute most marginalized of the most marginalized because that is not my life. What I can do though is witness the invisible and slowly build bridges towards what I can not see to invest resources beyond what I know and understand.

I claim the margins as my pathway for recognizing that the margins exist, they are deep, and as soon as I think I have found the edge I am actually just at the beginning. To know the margins of marginalizations is to name that we do not know the margins. My role, within and outside the margins is to extend the power I have onto others who are able to reach farther and farther out, allowing the most marginalized of the most marginalized to always lead the way.

I might be a trans, disabled, autistic, queer, displaced Indigenous Palestinian, Muslim, refugee, who recently became a Global North citizen but there is always someone else more marginalized. There is a Black, trans, disabled, autistic, queer, displaced Indigenous Palestinian, Muslim, refugee who is not a Global North citizen out there and my responsibility is to support them.

But the margins are not exclusively about listing out marginalized identities and saying this one is more marginalized than the other. Perhaps the person in the example has access to wealth that I do not, or our disabilities are marginalized in different ways. There is no exact formula. However, there is always someone more marginalized than we are.

When I walk into a room and I am the most marginalized within it my role is to ensure that I am not the end of the margins. My role is to be mindful of who is not there and build pathways for them to not only be in the room but perhaps have a completely separate room. But **if the margins end with me and I claim the role of the token, then only those in similar margins of those in the room will benefit.**

You might be wondering how someone who is the most marginalized in a room can do this work. Marginalization is also just one part of understanding power. Inherent power still exists regardless of marginalization. I am often the most marginalized person walking into a room when we start but I am also often the most powerful as discussed in earlier chapters. My understanding of the margins and my awareness of my power allow me to no longer be the most marginalized person in the room.

I do not do my work so people like me can benefit. I do my work so people who are far more marginalized benefit. I find that often, work is done for those we know, not all the people we will never know. That is the difference between collectivism and individualism. From an individualistic standpoint we may support and be with some at the margins of marginalization if we are at some of those same margins, but still we will not be *in service* to anyone more marginalized. This happens often within marginalized groups, creating our own small barriers that end up exclusionary to those more marginalized and allow us as marginalized communities to harm one another.

This is also why the most marginalized are the most fit to lead. Even an individualistic person at the margins is most likely more equipped to do liberation work than privileged individuals who are "collectivist". I put collectivism in quotations here because collectivism is a spectrum, and you may call yourself collectivist but unless you are *in service* to the most marginalized of the most marginalized your collectivism is actually just individualism branded for a woke world.

I am often asked about the notion to always center the voices of the most marginalized of the most marginalized. We are not centering the most marginalized of the most marginalized simply to center specific identities—we center the most marginalized of the most marginalized because individuals on the margins are the individuals who understand systemic oppression and worldbuilding better than anyone else. On the margins you see all the inner circles, you become an expert in navigating and managing individuals with privilege. The wisdom needed to build a liberated world is the priority—that wisdom is not exclusive to those on the margins, nor is it a given that just because someone is marginalized that they have this wisdom. Single identities and even intersectional identities do not capture our lived experience and definitely do not capture our lived wisdom.

To assume that every Palestinian has the same wisdom is tokenization and ultimately harms us all. To assume that even every trans Palestinian who might carry my exact identities is the same, is harmful. We do not control our lived experience, and there are no two people with the exact same experience. Wisdom is developed through action, in how we move in the world. Even members of the same families will not have the same wisdom, because as we move in the world we interact with things differently. We are meant to be different. We need our differences to create the conditions to belong, to be able to build a liberated world. But not all marginalized people have worldbuilding wisdom. There is an assumption that humans have always hated others who are different from them, but if that were true then we would have gone extinct. We have always needed individuals with different skill sets and experiences to support us in surviving and worldbuilding. A group of the exact same people can never survive, let alone thrive.

Center the most marginalized of the most marginalized, but to be *in service* to the most marginalized of the most marginalized is to honor wisdom.

I have been in far too many spaces where a marginalized person will be centered AND they will not have worldbuilding wisdom or any skill sets needed for liberation organizing. The reason this happens is because we tokenize the most privileged of the most marginalized. We rely on identities instead of experience and wisdom.

To be *in service* to the most marginalized of the most marginalized is to always center individuals on the margins who have the **right** experience and wisdom. To center someone who does not is reckless and harmful, impacting our movements in ways most people can barely begin to name, yet we see happen everyday.

There are far too many examples of individuals with the right identities being thrown into roles that do not fit their skill sets and wisdom. When they make the wrong decision, they are rarely held by community and told they are wrong due to identity politics. When things go badly afterwards then individuals blame movement spaces for the failure, when in fact it was a collective failure by everyone in the space start to finish.

An individual's experience may have taught them to be a wonderful mobilizer, not an organizer or strategist. Some are visionaries and not mobilizers. We all have different roles and when we do not know our roles we cause harm. Centering a marginalized individual without understanding roles is tokenizing at best, it is harmful.

When this occurs my role is to support individuals in understanding their roles while alleviating the possibilities of harm. My focus is never to punish. Being *in service* to one another is not about punishment, it is about working together to be *in service* to liberation. None of us are perfect! Everyone has a role to play and we do not dispose of individuals regardless. If individuals insist on being harmful, that would have been a different intervention. Even then, we do not punish, we do not dispose of. However, I will make their power irrelevant to ensure harm can not occur, and when they are ready to move towards accountability the door is open to a space filled with support to allow them to grow into that accountability.

Our commitment is to collective liberation, not a single individual. If you are marginalized and you do not have worldbuilding wisdom then why would I center you in a space where that wisdom is necessary? This doesn't mean individuals are not valid or we hate them or anything else, it just means they have a different role to play.

Be *in service* to collective liberation first and foremost, everything else is to guide us towards that goal.

HOW WE LIVE
OUR LIVES
MATTERS

In Service to Community Care

If we are *in service* to community, to liberation, to land, to spirit, to the revolution, then are we not always *in service* to community care? The short answer is yes. This answer applies to all of these areas of service, only broken down for the sake of accessibility, but ultimately are one and the same. We can not be *in service* to liberation without being *in service* to community care. But that doesn't mean that's what actually happens.

I have learned about the concept of community care through many names in my adulthood and through living it as a child. Then came into it as an adult through peer support. Peer support offers a framework that recognizes that we all need support, and we are capable of providing support.

In 2020, discourse changed to include mutual aid as the mainstream form of community care. "Mutual" is meant to honor reciprocity, yet reciprocity is often neglected within the vast majority of mutual aid networks. This is partially due to the privilege that many mutual aid organizers carry in not being of the margins and their own unconscious bias of what those on the margins can provide as forms of support. Ultimately, the majority of mutual aid is about ego, for if that were not the case it would be called charity or resource redistribution. Many want to claim mutual aid without being *in service* to community care.

All areas of being are areas that can be *in service* to the ego or *in service* to the areas themselves. Being *in service* to mutual aid is very different from being a part of mutual aid. You can be a part of mutual aid and still be *in service* to ego, or worse, fascism. I did not call this chapter *in service* to mutual aid because I am not *in service* to mutual aid, I am *in service* to community care and that can include mutual aid as a pathway but is not exclusive to it. I highlight this again and again because to me it is not about what you brand something, rather it is about how we are *in service*.

To be *in service* to community care is to honor that we all need support, which requires me to be ready and willing to accept all forms of support. It means that I am moving beyond the belief that I can only do this on my own.

To be *in service* to community care is to honor that everyone is capable of providing support, which means that I am ready and willing to receive support also. It also means that I prevent the barriers from others being able to provide support, ensuring that no one is robbed of reciprocity.

To be *in service* to community care is to honor that we all need support and are able to provide it and that looks very different within a liberated world compared to a systemically oppressive one. This means that as I am *in service*, I recognize that community care will take on many different forms and to be *in service* to the most marginalized of the most marginalized means that I am not the one dictating what that care needs to look and feel like.

This is why community care can include: charity, resource redistribution, land back, mutual aid, reparations, and so many other forms of support.

Charity

Charity is often seen as an elitist form of support—this is true, butjust because we don't like the word doesn't mean that the concept has disappeared or that the concept has no place in community care.

Charity comes from systemically oppressive hierarchical societies where elites are taught that by giving to those "less fortunate souls" then they are "good" people. Charity is not relational, so it is the most privileged determining the type of support, the timing, and everything else. There may not seem like there is much space for charity in liberation work but there is space for everything. If we know a rich billionaire wants to give a blond white person tens of millions of dollars and we mobilize that blond white person to give us the money so we may redistribute it, how much does it matter that this person is just trying to feel "good"? Charity is often the backbone of resource redistribution. We don't give the credit to the billionaire whose entire wealth is stolen and has probably stolen more in the time it takes for the millions of dollars to reach anyone. However, those are resources that are now in the community. This is also not mutual aid, there is no reciprocity, and there is no intention to dismantle the systems that allowed the theft in the first place.

Resource Redistribution

Resource redistribution is when we redistribute stolen resources back to the communities they were stolen from. It is not about those of us doing the redistribution and it is not about preventing further theft—that becomes mutual aid. The main difference between charity and resource redistribution is political analysis. In resource redistribution the individuals involved know that money was stolen and needs to be returned. In charity, it is an act of unnecessary niceness to give resources away. The same example above for charity can extend to resource redistribution when it is redistributed by the blond white person we had mobilized. They were mobilized because they were able to recognize that this is stolen money.

There can be a lot of ego in both charity and resource redistribution. Charity is always built on ego and chasing a feeling of "goodness" and the same can apply to resource redistribution. Resource redistribution recognizes the theft and that returning resources is just that, returning something stolen. However, many still feel a sense of "goodness" because they knew to return stolen resources. There are many white people I know who will support others in returning stolen resources but will not return the stolen resources they are hoarding.

Reparations and land back are both specific forms of resource redistribution to address specific harm to and theft from Black and Indigenous communities.

Resource redistribution is a way to support others in surviving capitalism so that we may be able to truly invest in practices like mutual aid. It also allows us to begin relationship building which is essential for mutual aid.

Mutual Aid

Mutual aid is where politics, culture, and The Revolution meet resource redistribution. Our needs are not met because systems of oppression intentionally ensure that we do not have what we need to rise up and build a liberated world. Scarcity is a tool of systems of oppression. We are meant to be overwhelmed, to suffer, and ultimately perish under the weight of imperialism. Charity does not need to acknowledge this reality, and resource redistribution only acknowledges systems of oppression so far as to say that we are not surviving. Mutual aid recognizes that our needs are not met by design and a world where our needs are met is possible—and it's our role to build it.

Mutual aid requires a culture shift to recognize the true value of being human beyond capitalist white supremacy. As humans, we are meant to be in reciprocal relationships, receiving and providing support to one another. As humans, we have lived millennia without white supremacy and capitalism, we will live millennia more without them. Mutual aid requires a return to who we were prior to systems of oppression and an invitation towards who we will be after them.

Mutual aid is a practice of supporting one another to meet our needs while we work to build a liberated world by dismantling the systems of oppression that created the conditions of why we need care to begin with. But care does not begin or end with systems of oppression. Care is human. Care exists in every type of world we create while oppression is not a part of every reality we can create. Mutual aid is care that works specifically to uproot and dismantle systems of oppression.

Mutual aid requires an understanding of how our needs are impacted due to systems of oppression, and of how we are oppressed in different ways to ensure we do not build a better world. Mutual aid requires an understanding of power and marginalization. Systems of oppression impact us all differently, and not just differently across identities, they impact us differently across time and location and even the industries we are in to survive capitalism. Since our marginalization and privilege are constantly in flux within systems of oppression, mutual aid requires relationships beyond our levels of marginalization and privilege.

Often, mutual aid is said to start between neighbors and family. Sure, the start of mutual support may begin interpersonally. However, mutual aid is not just mutual support, it is about dismantling the circumstances that led to the injustice of stealing and hoarding resources. If jeff bezos and elon musk gave each other sugar as neighbors that is not mutual aid. If I live in an upper middle class neighborhood and we carpool our children together that is not mutual aid, but it can be.

In the example with the blond white person we can take those resources to invest in pathways to disrupt the theft of resources beyond just giving stolen money back to the most marginalized.

Mutual aid is a transformative worldbuilding practice for the most marginalized of the most marginalized that disrupts the theft of resources by systems of oppression and those that serve them. When I say disrupts, I mean mutual aid serves as an investment in alternative systems where we get our needs met collectively. Current care systems within systems of oppression ensure we remain insecure culturally, materially, and financially. We are conditioned to uphold systems of oppression in the culture these systems create around care.

To access care within white supremacist imperialist patriarchal capitalism you must cater to the most privileged to receive support. You must sell a story that fits neatly into these systems and that empowers the benefactors of these systems as saviors. The system enforces a scarcity practice, pitting those in need of support against one another and creating hierarchies that reinforce our marginalizations. This creates a culture of competitiveness, lack of worth, and self-blame for our marginalization.

Mutual aid is meant to transform this culture to a culture of care and support where we all get our needs met and in the process build a better world.

You can not be *in service* to mutual aid and *in service* to systems of oppression at the same time. If you are in service to oppression, then you are doing charity or at best resource redistribution. Mutual aid is political and it is meant to be transformative.

A good litmus test for mutual aid is to reflect after it has been operating for several months about whether or not any circumstances have shifted. Does the community have more resources? Has the culture of support shifted? What do relationships look like? If there is no significant impact in any of these areas then it is not mutual aid.

The challenge with mutual aid within the levels of systemic oppression we are contending with is that the systems will often retaliate against mutual aid networks with state and community violence. If the community is always utilizing the little resources they have to support one another then we are not able to meet the immense needs that arise. Without resource redistribution and investing additional resources into our infrastructure so that it keeps supporting the community, often community members return to surviving capitalism in the ways that they had to prior.

Ultimately, if mutual aid does not become the dominant culture it will fail. When I say it fails I am not referring to a single network. This is where culture comes in. If I am in a mutual aid network with 50 people and it does not work out, that does not mean that my service to mutual aid ends, it just means that my mutual aid is no longer revolving around this ecosystem made of 50 people. Mutual aid is a lifelong practice and it does not need to be contained in a network, it is how we live our lives. This is the difference between being *in service* and just being a part of something.

Mutual aid is not something we meet weekly about and discuss things. Mutual aid is in how you interact with everyone, every interaction is a part of dismantling systems of oppression.

Mutual aid starts with:

- understanding our needs
- why our needs are not met
- what needs need to be met strategically to allow us to work to dismantle these systems

Mutual aid requires:

- understanding systems of oppression
- understanding power, privilege, and marginalization
- understanding scarcity culture
- understanding liberation culture

Mutual aid is maintained through:

- relationships
- material, emotional, physical, and spiritual care for one another
- community investment

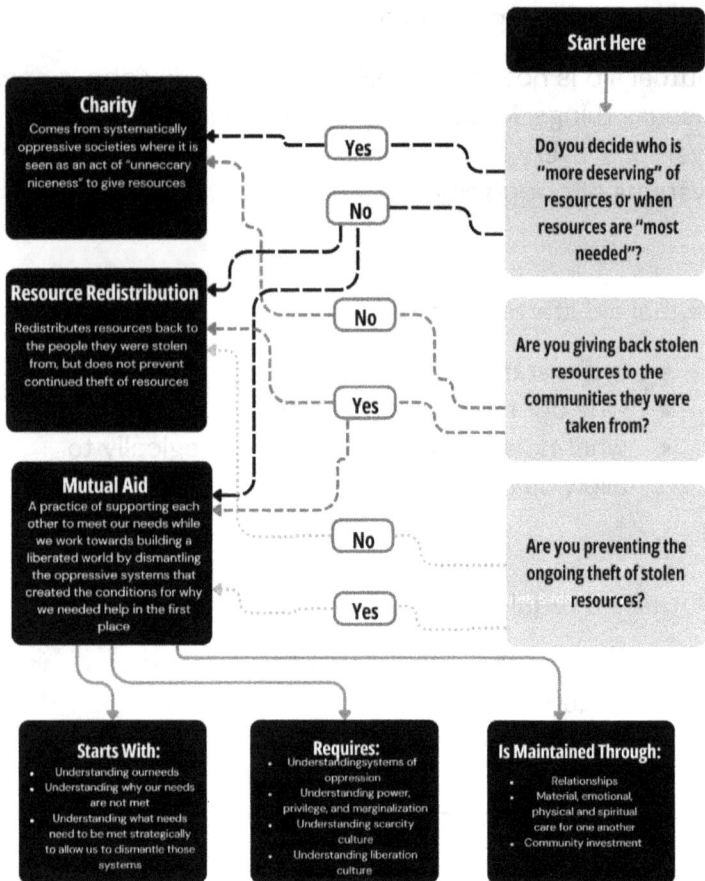

Start Here

Do you decide who is "more deserving" of resources or when resources are "most needed"?

Yes →

Charity
Comes from systematically oppressive societies where it is seen as an act of "unneccary niceness" to give resources

No →

Are you giving back stolen resources to the communities they were taken from?

No →

Resource Redistribution
Redistributes resources back to the people they were stolen from, but does not prevent continued theft of resources

Yes →

Are you preventing the ongoing theft of stolen resources?

No →

Mutual Aid
A practice of supporting each other to meet our needs while we work towards building a liberated world by dismantling the oppressive systems that created the conditions for why we needed help in the first place

Yes →

Starts With:
- Understanding ourneeds
- Understanding why our needs are not met
- Understanding what needs need to be met strategically to allow us to dismantle those systems

Requires:
- Understandingsystems of oppression
- Understanding power, privilege, and marginalization
- Understanding scarcity culture
- Understanding liberation culture

Is Maintained Through:
- Relationships
- Material, emotional, physical and spiritual care for one another
- Community investment

PATHWAYS TO COMMUNITY CARE

Illustration by Mishandi Sarhan

216

So, let's talk some examples.

Back to elon and jeff, sharing some sugar. No, that is not charity, resource redistribution, and definitely not mutual aid. A need is not always caused by systems of oppression. Charity, resource redistribution, and mutual aid are specifically related to needs created due to systemic oppression. Elon running out of sugar is not due to white supremacy.

But let's move past elon and jeff. Let's talk about two neighbors or friends in your city sharing sugar, flour, cookies, or even meals. This example applies to ride shares, child care, and so many other things that we may be supporting one another with. The first question we ask is why does this need exist? Is the need created specifically due to systemic oppression. If yes, then depending on how we support, it will fall into charity, resource redistribution, or mutual aid. If the answer is no, then this is just support. We love support, but not all support has to be labeled as some kind of radical form of worldbuilding.

If the need is in fact due to systems of oppression then we ask further questions about why this need exists in the first place and the positionality of who is providing support. For example, if one neighbor is working class and one is middle-class then that can easily create the conditions for charity. If one of the two is not impacted in that same way—in this example one neighbor is able to access sugar while the other can not—and the one who can access sugar gives some to their neighbor then that is charity. If the sugar is given with an understanding that the more affluent neighbor only has sugar because it is stolen then that becomes resource redistribution. If it ends there then we have not reached a level of mutual aid. However, if the neighbors recognize that this injustice exists beyond them and must be addressed beyond them then we are at the beginning stages of mutual aid. Once we begin addressing the barriers and creating infrastructure to address the systems of oppression creating these needs, then we are moving deeper into mutual aid work. When our mutual aid reaches individuals we will never know then we have truly moved towards creating a culture of mutual aid for our community.

Let's take another immediately relevant example. Many individuals worldwide are currently supporting families in Gaza impacted by the genocide caused by the apartheid zionist state. Most of the support is labeled as Mutual Aid, very little actually qualifies as mutual aid.

If you send money to families without a political analysis of how you are benefitting from this genocide then that is charity. If you send money from a place of distrust and a desire for controlling how the funds are spent and are demanding proof of how the funds are spent from people experiencing genocide then that is charity.

If you recognize that you benefit from the genocide and are sending funds to individuals impacted, honoring that only individuals with lived experience are the rightful decision makers, and not demanding labor from them then that is resource redistribution.

If you recognize that we all benefit from genocide and we must change the conditions of the world so that genocide never occurs again and you move towards building infrastructure to build that world, then we are moving towards mutual aid. I say towards mutual aid because mutual aid can be incredibly expansive.

Let's be more specific, with an example from my work.

Since Oct 7th, 2023 I have moved nearly a million u.s. dollars directly to trans and queer individuals most impacted by genocide; this includes individuals in Gaza, Sudan, Congo, Kashmir, and elsewhere. Most of my work is resource redistribution, some is mutual aid.

There is some money that I move that is just an acknowledgement of systemic oppression and is sent to individuals most impacted; this money is sent in unrestricted ways beyond me.

Mutual aid in my work is supporting individuals in Gaza and other genocide zones (or in other spaces globally) who are organizing to remove the barriers to getting our needs met. The support in Gaza for example is not just supporting a single person, it is supporting individuals and collectives who are building infrastructure to feed hundreds of individuals. Globally, the support is investing in trans and queer organizers most impacted by genocide who are actively (or will hopefully one day) do the liberation work needed to end all genocides.

To put it a little more clearly, mutual aid is a part of being in service to liberation. The service is front and center, not an afterthought, it is a requirement.

Charity, resource redistribution, and mutual aid are all different pathways within community care. Community care encompasses all of these various pathways and others as they are needed.

When we are *in service* to community care we are actively caring for one another. It is in the interactions and the energy I bring into spaces. It is in having faith in humans instead of fear of humans. Don't get me wrong I hate people often, but care has nothing to do with liking or hating. Care is something that we all deserve and play a role in.

We are living in a world where it feels like many have remembered to hate the bourgeoisie, the ruling class, the 1%. Yet, most can not name their hatred for individuals who are poor. Capitalism teaches us many things, some of which is that poverty is self-inflicted, and poverty is the worst thing you can ever experience. Capitalism teaches us it's okay to go through every abuse within capitalism as long as you don't become poor. This has resulted in a deep and profound hatred that most people can not and will not name. When we refuse to name this hatred and move away from it then we refuse to shut down the world for liberation. This is why the vast majority of people refuse to risk their jobs because we are taught capitalist work is our "livelihood", as if we will not live without capitalism. Our hatred of the poor, our terror of being poor keeps us immobilized. This terror also prevents us from truly being in community and accessing one another's wisdom. This is where mutual aid really comes in.

We can not truly practice mutual aid without addressing our terror of poverty and our hatred of individuals who are poor. Capitalism has sold itself to us as the only thing that can save us.

The ego tells us that care is different for loved ones or for ourselves compared with those that we do not know—yayyyyy patriarchy. Being *in service* to community care is recognizing that we are always caring for everyone, whether we know it or not. It recognizes that what we put into the universe is a part of the movement of currents that are felt everywhere. *In service* to community care is recognizing that care is something that exists beyond oppression and liberation, it is human, it will always be here and our role in it does not end ever.

If we define the community as more expansive than our inner circles of people we know and love then community care must be for everyone and everything, not just what we know.

There is a hadith that says that no one will enter heaven unless they wish for others what they wish for themselves. My litmus test for the people I know is not how they treat me, it's how they treat the people they don't know. If I only offer support to the people I am connected to then what happens to everyone deeper in the margins? Community care is a part of being *in service* to the most marginalized of the most marginalized.

When community care is *in service* to the most marginalized of the most marginalized then even if you are supported as an individual but your community is not, then you do not feel supported.

To be human is to be in community. If we are to move towards collective liberation we have to remember that it is only in community that collective liberation is possible.

These days there are a lot of people—more than ever—who like me. Many will show up if I ask them to, but they will not do the same for others like me that they do not know. I can not possibly feel supported if my people are not supported. I am *in service* to community care regardless of my personal connections.

I also use the language of community care because even in a liberated world community care will exist. We will always need to be *in service* to community care. We always have a role to play. Are you ready for your role in a liberated world?

WHEN NO ONE IS DISPOSABLE THEN EVERYONE IS CARED FOR

In Service to Truth, to Justice

"Seven fat cows eaten by seven lean cows, and seven green ears of grain and seven dry ones."

Dream interpretation by Yusif: "Seven years of prosperity. Followed by seven years of famine."

Surat Yusif, ayah 47-49

I had a dream mid January 2025 as soon as I moved to a different house. The dream is of seven cows killing seven others, and I am the 7th killed—referencing Surat Yusif (the story of Joseph). In the dream I am nonchalant about my death, for I know that the world is meant to end anyway. Death in dreams is often a new life. My aunt, the best dream interpreter I know, sent me a 9 minute voice note interpreting my vision. This dream is meant to symbolize a new chapter in my life: after decades of work, an old life will die and I will be transformed. I am writing this over two months later and I feel myself in that transformation process. I am finally in a place where I am comfortable with the process and at peace within myself. I will find who I am meant to be when I am meant to.

For months I have felt like I am being pulled in every direction, like my inner atoms are being realigned. My aunt told me to read Surat Yusif so that I may find some guidance and insight into my own journey. As soon as I heard the first few words I understood why I was called to revisit this Surah in the Quran.

Surat Yusif is one of my favorite chapters of the Quran. It is about 15 pages of storytelling, the full story from childhood to adulthood of Prophet Yusif. I used to love this surah in my adolescence and as a young adult; and now, as an adult, I am remembering why I loved it so much.

Surat Yusif starts with Yusif sharing with his dad Yaqoub (Jacob) a dream he has where he is surrounded by 11 planets and the sun and moon, and they all bow to him. Yaqoub tells him not to share this dream with his siblings for jealousy can be incredibly harmful.

The older siblings in fact were jealous of Yusif and together conspired a plan to get rid of him. They asked their dad for permission to take him with them on an outing. Yaquob says that he worries that they will be distracted and Yusif will be eaten by a wolf. They assured him that they will be watchful and protect their younger brother. They say, if the wolf does eat him then that's representative of who they are and they would surely be losers.

Later that evening the siblings come back crying, with sheep blood on Yusif's cloth and say we were distracted and the wolf ate him. The line that always strikes me is they say, without any accusations from Yaqoub, "and you would not have faith in us even if we were truthful".

I want to break down the dynamics here for there is a lot we can learn about families from these extreme interactions. We know the other siblings are older but do not know their actual ages. We know the siblings are so jealous of Yusif that they throw him in a well and assume he is dead. When I learned this story as a child it was said that Yusif was Yaqoub's favorite child. Now, Yaqoub is a prophet coming from a long line of prophets, yet potentially treats his children in a differential way that has created such animosity between the children.

At this point in the story (and my life) my intrigue and curiosity is about the siblings. On one hand you can experience pain from someone else receiving something that you desire. You come from a line of prophets and prophets are meant to be the best of people, enlightened. Yet in this case, it is someone enlightened that is the cause of your pain and I wonder what that does to your spirit. And by wonder I mean we know what that does to your spirit. I am conscious here not to place trauma of the 21st century on a story told 1500 years ago about people who lived over 3700 years ago and I want to stick with the facts listed out in the story from 1500 years ago in the Quran.

Yusif has a dream.

Warned about jealousy of siblings.

Siblings attempt to kill Yusif.

"and you would not have faith in us even if we were truthful"

This line blows my mind.

The biggest harm that any community members have ever done to me is not when I've been attacked with lies, it's when someone in power says in response, "we know it's not true and we don't want to address it". This speaks to bystander effects and abuses of power by people with enough power that justice and truth-seeking is reliant on their labor.

It is not always easy to do something. When I was 23 someone came to me telling me about financial abuse they witnessed by someone I was working with who was in her mid-40s. The person was coming to me because I had suggested the mid-40s individual as a speaker and she mismanaged some donation money. In a way, I was the link that allowed this problem to exist. I did not know what to do. I was barely surviving. The individual in their mid-40s by then had been severely abusing me and although the person approaching me did not know this I had no one to actually turn to for justice with this individual. I said I would do something. Instead I fled the country to survive away from this person. I think about this all the time. Someone reached out for support and I was not able to support them. There were many factors at play here, but I have been on the other side and abandonment by a trusted person festers and harms everyone involved eventually.

This same individual, the mid-40s Brown cis woman has harmed more individuals than I might ever know, she has led to suicide attempts, deportations, loss of housing, loss of jobs, and complete ostracization from community—and these are just the instances I know of, including my own. I became unhoused for 18 months and lost my entire community due to this individual. I could not stop this person when the first red flag was brought forward. However, there are countless others within the community, elders and friends of this individual in positions of power who have never responded when any of us have asked for support. This was between 2015 and 2017 and since then I have seen this happen in every community I support—dozens of communities.

adrienne maree brown has a book called *We Will Not Cancel Us*. I am incredibly tempted to publish a book called *We Have Already Canceled Us, Now What?*

I keep going back to the line "and you would not have faith in us even if we were truthful". In an age where the truth is political and facts don't matter, truth and faith are no longer connected. *Be Better Broken* was written in response to community violence and the response 99% of the time to the individuals causing harm was "well they're not okay". Justice is built on the entire truth, not a singular part of the truth. A singular part of the truth ultimately is a lie.

In Yusif's story, Yaqoub knows the truth. The siblings know the truth. Yusif knows the truth. Yet, injustice still occurs. Yusif is still thrown into a well. At every step, everyone allowed it to happen, rendering the truth irrelevant.

The same exact cycle of truth and injustice is in the second half of Yusif's story.

Yusif is found and bought into the chief minister's family in Egypt where "he may be of use or can be claimed as our child" as the chief minister says to his wife, far from home in Falasteen where Yusif's family is.

The story is that Yusif grows to be beautiful, so beautiful that the chief minister's wife attempts to seduce him and he runs from her and she tears his shirt from the back as he runs. When caught she says that he tried to rape her. One of her family members investigating said to see how his shirt was torn, if from the front then he is lying and she is truthful, if from the back she is lying and he is truthful. He was truthful, yet there is no accountability. She is asked to repent and reflect on what she's done, but nothing changes.

After, angered that the women in town were talking about her, she invites them over, gives them knives to cut vegetables and asks Yusif to come to them. When they see him they cut their fingers off, hypnotized by his beauty. She tells him that unless he sleeps with her she will imprison him. He chooses prison. Thus, despite the earlier attempt that many are aware of and despite many in attendance, the injustice still occurs.

I pause here to reflect on this. Although many knew the truth, even with proof, the marginalized individual was punished anyway. The truth became what the majority wanted it to be and injustice occurred. Even though everyone knew the truth, Yusif was still imprisoned. How often do the many know the truth and allow the injustice to continue out of malice, ignorance, boredom, or convenience?

Yusif is imprisoned for years. His two cellmates have dreams that he interprets. The first is to be executed, the other is to serve as a servant to the king.

Yusif is imprisoned for some more years until the king has a dream and the cellmate says that Yusif can interpret it. Yusif is requested to interpret the dream and he does sofrom his cell. Intrigued, the king calls for him. Yusif refuses the audience with the king until the truth is revealed by the women who led to Yusif's incarceration.

The chief minister's wife and the others are brought forward. At first they deny the claim until the chief minister's wife says that it is time for the truth to come out and exonerates him. In fact she says, "I say this so Yusif knows that I have not betrayed him behind his back and God does not forgive those who betray. I do not exonerate myself for the ego strives for badness except what My Lord prevents, My Lord is forgiving". There is a sense of repentance, but does it count when years have passed and this truth comes out only because the king demanded it, because Yusif refused to see him without it? Does the king actually care? Who is actually cognizant of justice other than Yusif? Is anyone in service to truth and justice?

Yusif asks to be in charge of all commerce to manage the crises foretold in the king's dream.

One day Yusif's siblings arrive in Egypt to trade. Yusif refuses them, knowing who they are, and asks them to bring him their youngest brother who was back home with Yaqoub. They go back and request the youngest to travel with them and Yaqoub says he fears that he will end up like Yusif, but allows them to take him anyway.

When they get back to Yusif he hides a chalice in the youngest brother's bag and calls them thieves and imprisons the youngest asking them to return with their father. He tells the youngest brother who he is and that he is safe. He tells the other siblings that they must be accountable for their actions with him, they recognize who he is, and they return with Yaqoub. The eleven of them, Yaqoub, and Yusif's mother bow to him, fulfilling the dream of 11 planets and the sun and moon.

As a child, the epilogue (as told by adults, not in the Quran) was that the siblings, Yaqoub, and the mom all move to Egypt.

I hold onto this story today and within the dream that I had—which was similar to the dream of the King—recognizing the harm that happens when injustice occurs and the truth is known. There are many times when the truth is not known, but there are many times when it does not matter.

I connect to the story today because of my own experiences with cis women as an adult. Every cis woman (except for two) who I refused to sleep with, be in a relationship with, or marry told me I was leading them on and that I was violent. These are not steps 1-3, this is cis women wanting us to skip the first two and get married immediately. This was at a time when I was healing from childhood sexual assault and refused very publicly to sleep with anyone, date anyone, or marry anyone. And being queer, I was told I was the problem, even when I was sexually assaulted by drunk cis women. The truth didn't matter, the optics did, power did.

This past year, in 2024, a cis woman told me she likes me. I told her I am in a position of power and can not even consider her a possibility. She claimed I was denying her autonomy to make her own decision. She said I had triggered her and her therapist agrees that I am harmful to the community. To me this was a very straightforward situation, and I will not debate basic ethics. Some things are not up for debate for me, and I refuse to compromise in an area where we want to pretend as if lines do not exist. Because in most spaces lines do not exist. Either the truth is not known or the truth is known and it doesn't matter. Justice happens when the truth matters.

I share the experiences from 2015-2017 in recognition that years later, I am holding onto this injustice more than any other injustices in my life, because it was this experience that complicated the relationship between truth and justice for me. Prior, my autistic mind believed that if people believed the truth and we had the power to shift things then justice happens. This new understanding shifted everything for me, because so much organizing, as I understood it, was about shifting power to achieve justice. But if the truth does not matter, then regardless of the power we build we will not have justice.

We see this in many communities. Systemically oppressive power is constantly in flux, yet in many places as power is gained we actually move towards more injustice.

Being *in service* to justice requires us to be *in service* to truth, recognizing that the truth alone does not lead to justice. The truth alone can lead to further injustice.

If we are not *in service* to justice then being *in service* to truth does not matter.

Being *in service* to justice means that regardless of how inconvenienced we are we dedicate our actions to it. Injustice is an open wound that festers and grows and spreads. Every time we do not show up *in service* to justice things only get worse. If I had shown up for the first person who contacted me we may have been able to close the wound that ultimately would go on to harm countless others, including the person who came to me, me, and nearly everyone we knew in that community. I didn't know what to do and I invest in myself and my community every day to know what to do next time or for someone around me to be able to show up when I fail to.

I yearn for us to close more of these wounds. I believe we need to name these wounds, skill build to know how to hold one another, and to ultimately do the work for justice to close the wounds of injustice and allow us to heal together. We can not be *in service* to liberation or the revolution or anything else if we are not *in service* to justice.

****

Conclusion,

I feel as if we are often forgetting that all the work is meant to lead us somewhere. Every struggle, every trauma, every experience is meant to lead us somewhere, and they are caused by something. In the context of capitalist white supremacist society we suffer due to systemic oppression and we are meant to move towards liberation. To my autistic brain (which I recognize is not necessarily your brain, dear reader) the world that we currently endure fits neatly within the spectrum ranging from systemic oppression to liberation. Of course, this is but a small spectrum in comparison to the reality of everything that we are and are meant to be. Life exists before and after systemic oppression—we exist beyond liberation. The world is so much more than what we live through every day, yet until we are liberated we may only visit this world as if it's fantasy. I want to live in that world. I want all of us to live in that world—the one beyond systemic oppression, the one beyond the desperate need for liberation. I say desperate because we will die otherwise.

I find power in that simplicity. I find conviction in that simplicity. I find myself in that simplicity and glimpse the world that could have been—the world that will be. If that's too poetic for you then I hope you find actual concrete thoughts throughout the book. To end, let me be poetic, let me dream and hope, let me live worlds through words even if I never find my way into them.

May we all find our way there—wherever there begins and ends. May these words aid you on your journey.

May you be better broken. May you be *in service* to liberation—always.

A WORLD WHERE OUR NEEDS ARE MET IS POSSIBLE

Dear Reader,

Yes, you. Yes, no I'm serious, like you who is reading these words, whoever you are. Until this point, you may have been visualizing other people that this book is written about. It is not written for them, it is written for you.

We can all be the problem. We are all the problem. Nearly every person I wrote this book to specifically will assume this book is not for them—rendering this book entirely useless because of the deflection.

Start with "I am the problem."

Then expand from there.

Not only can we all be the problem but unless every single one of us pivots and shifts we will not move towards a liberated world. If someone harms me and I do not change in any way then I have wasted a growth opportunity.

Reread this, entirely open to receiving it about yourself. Until then, we are stuck. Break the cycle.

Be better broken.

JUSTICE HAPPENS WHEN THE TRUTH MATTERS

Acknowledgements

It has gotten harder and harder to write acknowledgements after each book. The time in between a reminder of all who were lost along the way, due to being killed, disappeared, burned out, and due to conflict. There is an immense amount of grief in between each book, even as I sit in deep gratitude for the support I receive from so many.

There is and will always be endless gratitude to Andrea Ramos and Mays Salamah for their work behind the scenes in making this book a reality. Thank you to Mishandi Sarhan for creating the beautiful flow chart representing community care.

Deep gratitude for Ijeoma Oluo, for gifting me and everyone reading these words a brilliant foreword—truly a dream. Your work has been and will always be a guiding light in my service to liberation.

This work would not have been complete without the stunning artwork of Sheyam Ghieth, who was able to capture the vision of these words and share them in the most beautiful artwork.

Immense gratitude to everyone doing the work and everyone who will be in the work. May you find the guidance you need along the way.

Gratitude to so many others, many of whom are no longer with us, and by the time these words reach you, many others will not be with us. Gratitude for the grief and gratitude for the short overlap of our lives, may we all be liberated, always.

About Yaffa

Photo by Andrea Ramos Campos

Mx. Yaffa is an author, organizer, and culture worker. Yaffa's poetry, non-fiction, and speculative fiction books have been sold globally and translated to various languages. Yaffa's service to liberation spans continents and dozens of communities. They dream of living in a liberated world where they can be 'the messy one'.

About Meraj Publishing

Meraj Publishing is a Disabled Trans Palestinian Muslim owned rapid response publishing house that centers Trans global majority voices impacted by genocide. Recognizing the vast inequities in the publishing industry and the often long processes to have a work published. Meraj aims to publish writing by individuals most impacted as soon as possible to inform the on the ground organizing and worldbuilding needs. Meraj prioritizes stories that focus on organizing, worldbuilding, building utopia, hope, love, spirituality, and belonging. Meraj Publishing is entirely run and operated by Trans and Queer global majority individuals.

www.ingramcontent.com/pod-product-compliance
Lightning Source LLC
Chambersburg PA
CBHW052125270326
41930CB00012B/2758